The
Templemore
Miracles

'The age of miracles is not past – go to Templemore'

Tipperary Star, 20 August 1920

THE TEMPLEMORE MIRACLES

JIMMY WALSH, CEASEFIRES AND MOVING STATUES

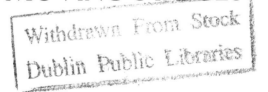

JOHN REYNOLDS

The
History
Press

First published 2019

The History Press
97 St George's Place, Cheltenham,
Gloucestershire, GL50 3QB
www.thehistorypress.co.uk

British Library Cataloguing in Publication Data.
A catalogue record for this book is available from the British Library.

ISBN 978 0 7509 9059 2

Typesetting and origination by The History Press
Printed and bound in Great Britain by TJ International Ltd.

CONTENTS

ℐNTRODUCTION

In the aftermath of the 1916 Easter Rising and subsequent execution of the leaders of that rebellion, Irish Republicans moved relentlessly towards open conflict with the British Empire. Hostility between the Royal Irish Constabulary (RIC) and militant activists gradually escalated, culminating in the Soloheadbeg ambush of 21 January 1919 near a quarry in South Tipperary. Two constables of the RIC, James McDonnell and Patrick O'Connell, were shot dead by members of the 3rd Tipperary Brigade of the Irish Republican Army (IRA) as they escorted a consignment of explosives to the quarry. While there had been sporadic attacks on the RIC since 1916, the Soloheadbeg ambush had a new element of ruthlessness which distinguished it from attacks of previous years. The brutal nature of the ambush came as a shock to many moderate members of Sinn Féin and the Volunteer movement, as well as the wider population, not only in Ireland but internationally. The *Daily News* reported on the wider significance of the killings and what might result from them, stating that the 'well-meaning idealists in *Dáil Éireann* were utterly unable to control the physical-force men in the provinces'. The Soloheadbeg ambush also caused profound shock within the RIC and was viewed as an ominous escalation in the recent pattern of attacks on the police, and as a sign of approaching danger.

The Soloheadbeg ambush acted as a catalyst for many activists who had grown disillusioned with politics and believed that military action was the way to achieve an Irish Republic. A full-scale guerrilla war ensued, and having been a garrison town since 1813, Templemore was at the epicentre of events in Tipperary. When violence reached a peak during the summer of 1920, a series of extraordinary events occurred in Templemore and the nearby townland of Curraheen near the village of Gortagarry. James Walsh, a 16-year-old farm labourer, claimed that he was experiencing Marian apparitions, and that religious statues owned by him were moving and bleeding. He also said that a 'holy well' had sprung up in the floor of his bedroom. Miraculous cures were attributed to Walsh, and the religious fervour which subsequently gripped the area led to an influx of thousands of pilgrims from all over Ireland and abroad. The phenomenon of the 'Templemore Miracles', or 'bleeding statues of Templemore', lasted for several weeks. A bizarre situation arose as an informal ceasefire came into effect while both sets of combatants and the wider civilian population struggled to comprehend the surreal circumstances which existed. After several weeks, local IRA commanders interrogated Walsh, concluding that the so-called miracles and apparitions were not genuine. They also decided that the multitude of pilgrims coming to the area each day must be stopped as it was having a detrimental effect on their military operations. The IRA inquiry reached the highest level of the Republican hierarchy, with the direct involvement of Michael Collins. Deliberate, decisive and violent action was taken to deal with Walsh and to stop visitors from coming to Templemore. When the last pilgrims had departed, the conflict resumed in earnest, with a greater level of ferocity and brutality than previously. This book provides a comprehensive account of the supposed 'Templemore Miracles' which transfixed Ireland and gained worldwide notoriety and attention during the late summer of 1920.

VIOLENCE: 'THE TOWN IS A WRETCHED PLACE'[1]

Travelling into Templemore along any of the roads which encircle this small town, the skyline is dominated by the bell tower, accommodation blocks and of Richmond Barracks, the vast military complex built in the early years of the nineteenth century. On 22 October 1808, notices were placed in Irish newspapers by the commissioner of garrisons in Ireland, Major General Freeman, seeking proposals for the building of new infantry barracks at Parsonstown in Kings County (now Birr, County Offaly) and Templemore in Tipperary.[2] An intensive programme of barrack-building had begun following successful revolutions in America in 1776 and France in 1789. The revolutionary fervour which followed inspired a new generation of home-grown insurrectionists in Ireland, which culminated in the 1798 Rising and the United Irishmen rebellion of 1803 led by Robert Emmet. Aside from the fear of further uprisings, England was at war with

France and the threat of invasion from the army of Napoleon was a possibility, given that French fleets had arrived at Bantry Bay in 1786 and Killala Bay in 1798.[3]

To guard against invasion, over forty Martello towers were constructed around the coast, and between 1789 and 1814 the strength of the military garrison in Ireland increased from 40,000 to 225,000.[4] Sir Arthur Wellesley, the Duke of Wellington, commented on the positive attitude of Irish landowners towards the building of new barracks in their area, saying that the establishment of a barracks not only afforded a prospect of security, but 'required the expenditure of a large sum of money immediately, and if occupied by troops, the outlay in the neighbourhood of their subsistence and maintenance'.[5] In 1809 Sir Robert Peel, member of parliament for Cashel in Tipperary and the politician who would subsequently introduce a constabulary to rural Ireland, attributed the high level of disorder in the country to 'a natural predilection for outrage and a lawless life which I believe nothing can control'.[6] Making reference to the county which he represented in the House of Commons, Peel stated, 'You can have no idea of the moral depravation of the lower orders in that county … in fidelity towards each other they are unexampled, as they are in their sanguinary disposition and fearlessness of the consequences.'[7]

Peel was also harshly critical of the influence of the Roman Catholic Church, believing that the dominant religion of Ireland operated as an 'impediment rather than an aid to the ends of the civil government'.[8]

In 1804 the decision was made to build a large new barracks in Thurles, adjacent to the Ursuline convent which had been founded in 1799. Believing that the presence of a garrison so close to her school would be undesirable, Mother Clare Ursula, the head of the Order, wrote to Dublin Castle to protest, saying that she would close the school if the barracks was built beside it. On 10 November 1804, the Lord Lieutenant's secretary replied to Mother Clare Ursula, stating, 'His Excellency, having taken the facts therein set forth into consideration has been pleased to agree that the scite [sic] of the intended barracks at Thurles shall be changed, and has issued the necessary orders accordingly.'[9]

Following this exchange of correspondence, the decision was taken that the new barracks would instead be built in Templemore. Construction began in February 1809 and had been completed by 1813 at a total cost of £42,500, some £500 under budget. The Peninsular War, largely fought between the French and English, with armies led by Napoleon Bonaparte and the Duke of Wellington respectively, was in progress while the barracks was being built. To commemorate British military victories in that conflict, streets in Templemore were named after locations in Portugal connected with those victories. This resulted in somewhat exotic names being applied to places in a small town in North Tipperary, such as Wellington Mall, Talavera, Vimiero

Mall and Busaco Street. The barracks itself was named Richmond in honour of Charles Gordon-Lennox, the fifth Duke of Richmond, who served on the staff of the Duke of Wellington during the Peninsular War. It was built on a 57-acre site owned by local landowner Sir John Craven Carden (1757–1820).

In 1816 Captain Thomas Borrow and 800 soldiers of the West Norfolk Militia marched to Templemore from Clonmel barracks. Borrow's son, George, accompanied his father and lived in the barracks with him. George subsequently became a well-known author and in his book *Levengro* he described Richmond as a 'large military station, situated in a wild and thinly inhabited country ... extensive bogs were in the neighbourhood'. He referred to notable local landmark the 'Devil's Bit' mountain as 'exhibiting in its brow a chasm or vacuum, just for all the world as if a piece has been bitten out, a feat which, according to the tradition of the country, had actually been performed by his Satanic majesty'.[10]

When completed, Richmond was one of the largest military complexes in Ireland, with accommodation for fifty-four officers, 1,500 men and thirty horses, an eighty-bed hospital, a prison, fever hospital and dispensary.[11] Richmond was vitally important to the local economy, not only providing employment but also supporting local businesses such as merchants, publicans and farmers who catered for the large garrison. The presence of Richmond also provided the opportunity for local men to enlist. The main function of the barracks was as a base for 'depot battalions', where regiments which had been overseas on campaign were posted for a period to recruit, train and then depart on campaign throughout the British Empire. Irishmen were considered good recruits, described by one military surgeon as 'physically and morally the best adapted for service', and they signed up in large numbers to accept the 'Queen's shilling'.[12] In the late Georgian and Victorian era, the British Army could not have managed without Irish recruits. In 1830, for example, 40,979 Irishmen were in the Army, a figure of over 42 per cent of the total strength.[13]

Having such a large military installation in the town also brought many of the problems for which garrison towns gained notoriety, including drunkenness and prostitution. In 1844, for example, it was reported that the Templemore constabulary found a local woman called Ellen Stapleton in a field near the barracks 'in a dying state from the effects of a wound inflicted on her thigh by two other women of bad character … she was conveyed to hospital but died the following day'.[14] In 1855 a dramatic court case took place in Templemore Assizes, during which it was alleged that local parish priest Father Fennell had gone around the town to:

seek out and chastise any of the females who so much infest garrison towns. On this occasion however he mistook the wife of a Private Logan from Richmond for a prostitute and assaulted her. This resulted in a £1 fine in the magistrate's court, and the case caused a great sensation locally.[15]

Writing about Irish garrison towns including Templemore in 1864, the novelist Charles Dickens referred to 'open noonday immorality and drunkenness, and nightly licentious revelling ... vice is out of doors wandering shameless and defiant through the streets'.[16]

In 1847 Harry Loft, a 16-year-old ensign in the 64th Regiment of Foot (2nd Staffordshire), was garrisoned in Templemore. In a letter to his mother at home in the town of Louth, Lincolnshire, he described Richmond as, 'Splendid barracks, with two large squares, and all the buildings three stories high.' The town itself, however, he described as 'a wretched place ... there is only one street with three or four respectable shops'.[17] During the late 1850s, many Irish soldiers were sworn in as members of the 'Fenian' movement, and in 1857 it was reported that the 11th Depot Battalion from Templemore had been moved to Newry and replaced by the 59th Regiment from Glasgow, as it was 'strongly suspected that the 11th was tainted with Fenianism'.[18]

The nineteenth century saw a large turnover of regiments passing through Richmond, but by 1909 the barracks had largely been vacated. Templemore Town Council wrote to the War Office in London pleading for the army to return as the town was suffering substantial economic difficulties because of their absence, but were informed that there was 'no prospect of troops

being quartered there in the near future'.[19] The outbreak of the Great War in August 1914 brought about
a reversal of this policy, however, and by October 1914,
Richmond had become a large prisoner of war camp,
holding over 2,300 German soldiers who had been
captured in France. This was the only place in Ireland
where German military prisoners were detained. The
PoWs were guarded by Irish soldiers of the 3rd Leinster
Regiment. In March 1915 the prisoners were rapidly
moved to camps in England when the Royal Irish
Constabulary received intelligence that local members
of the Irish Volunteers had formulated a plan to break
into the barracks and release the prisoners. Given the
connections which existed between Irish Republicans
and the German government, which included the
efforts of Roger Casement to form an 'Irish Brigade'
from Irish soldiers imprisoned in Germany, the hope
was that the Templemore PoWs would join in the
rebellion that was then being planned, which would
become the 1916 Easter Rising. Following their hasty
departure, Richmond became a large training barracks
for Irishmen who were joining the British Army in
huge numbers as the Great War progressed, primarily
from the Munster Fusiliers and the Leinster Regiment.

Following the unsuccessful 1916 Easter Rising,
the war correspondent Henry Nevinson wrote in
Atlantic magazine, 'We execute a worthless rebel, and
for Ireland a heroic saint emerges from the felon's
grave.'[20] Nevinson astutely predicted that the decision

to execute the key figures behind the Rising, including P.H. Pearse and James Connolly, would generate enormous sympathy and thus provide iconic figures to the Republican movement, who viewed them as martyrs. In Tipperary there had initially been little public support for the Rising, with the *Tipperary Star* newspaper describing it as 'inexplicable imbecility – how a body of men could embark on such a desperate enterprise passes common sense comprehension … it is the old story, everything lost, nothing gained'.[21]

Notwithstanding the absence of an insurrection in Tipperary at Easter 1916, two members of the RIC, Sergeant Thomas Rourke and Constable John Hurley, were shot dead on 25 April while trying to arrest Volunteer Michael O'Callaghan for making a 'seditious' speech near Tipperary town. Following this incident, O'Callaghan went on the run and fled to America. Tipperary militants such as Dan Breen and Seán Treacy, the men who subsequently took part in the Soloheadbeg ambush, regarded O'Callaghan as 'having saved the name of Tipperary during Easter week' through his actions.[22] Some militant nationalists concluded that their aspirations could only be achieved by what they termed 'positive military action'.[23] Nonetheless, in the immediate aftermath of the Rising, overt volunteer activity had actually diminished, and almost 2,000 men had been interned.[24] The public empathy which manifested itself after the executions of the 1916 leaders was capitalised on, however, and the Volunteers gradually reorganised, increasing in number and engaging openly in acts of defiance. During late 1916 and early 1917, those arrested after the Rising were released and returned home to a rapturous reception. In 1917 Sinn Féin clubs and additional Volunteer companies were formed in Tipperary, with commensurate sharp increases in Volunteer activity and membership.[25]

An uneasy peace prevailed, but in December 1917 one British military intelligence officer described the growing and increasingly militant nationalist movement as 'peculiarly well disciplined, in comparison with similar political organisations in the past'. He went on to say that drunkenness was almost unknown amongst those deeply implicated, and was apparently severely dealt with. He found this to be 'in sharp contrast to the usual state of things in similar movements'.[26] Tipperary proved to be fertile ground for recruitment to the militant movement, and during the conscription crisis of early 1918 parades and field exercises were frequently held and plans formulated for the acquisition of arms. In January 1918 the IRA adopted a new national brigade structure to replace the previous inefficient command system whereby hundreds of companies had reported individually to IRA GHQ in Dublin. Three brigades were formed in Tipperary, 1st (North) Tipperary, 2nd (Mid) Tipperary and 3rd (South) Tipperary. Brigade officers and staff were elected by the membership, and Volunteers such as Seán Gaynor felt that 'the tempo of the organisation was stepped up, and we got into our stride as a military force'.[27]

The Soloheadbeg ambush was undertaken in contravention of instructions which had been issued by IRA Chief of Staff Richard Mulcahy, thus causing tension between GHQ and those who carried it out. In later life, Mulcahy wrote that he 'frequently despaired' of Volunteers in south Tipperary as they failed to respond to his efforts at instilling military discipline.[28] He also believed that as the ambush had been undertaken entirely on the initiative of Tipperary Volunteers, they could not be endorsed by the IRA leadership, and if they were captured or killed by the police, it could not be acknowledged that they had acted with authority and they would therefore be branded as 'common murderers'.[29] Mulcahy ordered members of the ambush party, including Breen and Treacy, to leave Ireland and go to the United States, but they refused to do so. Following the intervention of Michael Collins, they went instead to Dublin and joined a group of IRA Volunteers known as 'the squad' who were ordered by Collins to carry out targeted assassinations of key military, political and police personnel. Collins believed that 'the sooner fighting is forced and a general state of disorder created throughout the country, the better it will be for the country. Ireland is likely to get more out of a general state of disorder than from a continuation of the situation as it now stands.'[30]

Following the electoral success of Sinn Féin in December 1918, which saw it take seventy-three parliamentary seats out of a possible 105, many Volunteers had grown frustrated with politics and were anxious to continue the struggle for independence which they believed had started with the Rising.[31] Militants were frustrated that the events of 1916 had not led to a full-scale rebellion, and also at their own lack of involvement in the Rising.[32] The conscription crisis of early 1918 had passed, and that factor, allied to significant electoral success for Sinn Féin, meant that less-militant members assumed primacy. During one brigade meeting at the end of 1918, Treacy was angered by the lack of enthusiasm displayed by some Volunteers for drill and parades, and asserted, 'If this is the state of affairs, we will have to kill somebody and make the bloody enemy organise us!'[33]

In December 1918 Volunteers in Templemore devised a plan to raid Richmond barracks and seize the contents of its arsenal, as weapons and ammunition were in critically short supply. While Richmond was a formidable complex, the Volunteers received intelligence that on Sunday afternoons it was customary for officers from the barracks to dine at Hickey's Hotel in the town while a military band played outside, and enlisted men went for walks in the surrounding countryside. This left the barracks virtually undefended. Sunday was therefore the obvious day for an attack. Plans were made to cut railway tracks and telephone lines before storming the barracks, but to the anger of local Volunteers, GHQ in Dublin refused approval for the operation.[34]

In January 1919 the name 'Irish Republican Army' was adopted by the Irish Volunteers. In Tipperary, as in many other counties, militant Republicans moved unavoidably towards conflict with the police and military. The formation of an aspirational counter-state commenced with the inaugural public meeting of Dáil Éireann in Dublin on 21 January 1919 at 3.30 p.m. This would prove to be an historic event, but was overshadowed by the Soloheadbeg ambush, which entirely by coincidence took place on the same day. On 31 January 1919, *An t-Óglách*, the journal of the Irish Volunteers, editorialised that, 'A state of war exists between Ireland and England … every volunteer is entitled to use all legitimate methods of warfare against the soldiers and policemen of the English usurper and to slay them if necessary.'

In Tipperary, as in many other counties throughout history, this declaration of war was put into operation with deadly consequences.

In July 1920, when the inspector general of the RIC issued his monthly report on the situation in Ireland, he reported that the entire county of Tipperary was in a disturbed state and that the efforts of Sinn Féin were 'almost wholly directed against the police to make life unbearable for them'.[35] He described Munster as the worst of all four provinces, with fifteen RIC men having been murdered during July alone. Referring to the IRA campaign of boycotting and intimidation, which resulted in the police having to commandeer food, he reported that the recent establishment of an alternative system of justice comprising Sinn Féin courts and Republican police was having a serious effect, and people who were previously loyal were now obliged to have recourse to such illegal tribunals. He cautioned that if this system were allowed to continue with impunity, 'the ordinary law of the realm would be set at nought'. [36]

As the conflict in Tipperary intensified, police rein- forcements were drafted into the county to augment the strength of districts including Templemore, which apart from the district headquarters station in Templemore also had barracks at Roscrea, Borrisoleigh, Clonakenny, Golding's Cross, Templetouhy, Templederry, Timoney, Gurtaderrybeg and Castle Otway. Policing was under the command of District Inspector William Harding Wilson. A native of Ballycumber in King's County, Wilson joined the RIC in 1882 as a consta- ble and advanced through the ranks before arriving in Templemore in 1912 as district inspector. Wilson had spent a period attached to the office of the RIC Inspector General in Dublin Castle, thus giving him involvement in what were later categorised as 'a good deal of political cases'.[37] As Wilson had been stationed in Templemore since 1912, he had an intimate knowl- edge of the local members of the Volunteers, Sinn Féin and the IRA, thus making him a significant opponent. In March 1918 Wilson and his counterpart from the Thurles area, District Inspector Michael Hunt, were involved in a mass arrest of Volunteers, including IRA Commandant Seán Gaynor of 1st Tipperary Brigade, who in later life recalled being 'hauled out of my bed at 4.00 a.m. by a large force of police under Hunt and Wilson'. Hunt had received a first-class commendation for his diligence in making arrests and disrupting Sinn Féin meetings.[38] Both he and Wilson became priority targets for the IRA.[39]

Commandant Patrick Kinnane was concerned by what he described as the 'villainy of Hunt and his unscrupulous and ruthless tactics'.[40] Commandant Jimmy Leahy felt that if Hunt continued to operate with impunity it could have disastrous results, and that killing him 'would have a salutary effect on other policemen who might be inclined to follow his example'.[41] On 23 June 1919, Hunt was shot dead at Liberty Square in Thurles by Volunteer Jim Stapleton, who, along with several other IRA men, had mingled with a large crowd returning from a race meeting in the town. Following the 'daring act by undisguised men', the crowd panicked and fled in all directions, allowing the killers to escape without difficulty.[42]

As Hunt lay dying on the roadway a considerable crowd collected about, 'jeering and laughing but did not assist'.[43] Leahy later stated that for some hours after the shooting, police in Thurles appeared to be nervous, but as the evening wore on they got drunk and took out their anger by 'beating up anyone who they could get their hands on, especially any supporter of Sinn Féin'.[44] At the inquest which took place in Richmond Barracks in Templemore on the following day, the jury returned a verdict of 'wilful murder by a person or persons unknown'.[45] County Inspector Mulliner of the RIC reported to Dublin Castle that the verdict had only been reached after considerable hesitation and a grudging expression of sympathy was made to the relatives of the deceased by the jurors.[46] RIC Deputy Inspector General Flower also attended the inquest and remarked on the 'noticeable absence of members of the public'.[47] Mulliner linked the death of Hunt to the deaths of other RIC members in ambushes at Knocklong and Soloheadbeg, which he described as the 'first blows' against the force.[48] Archbishop Harty of the Diocese of Cashel and Emly condemned the murder as a flagrant violation of the Fifth Commandment, 'thou shalt not kill', but also blamed the 'provocative action of the government and gave his opinion that the military domination of Ireland should cease at once'.[49] He finished his eulogy by saying that the deed 'was done in Thurles, but was not of Thurles'.[50]

On 26 June the Lord Lieutenant of Ireland sent a telegram to the government in London stating his belief that Sinn Féin was 'an organised club for the murder of police', and went on to demand that the movement in Tipperary should be proclaimed as an illegal organisation.[51] Notices appeared in local and national newspapers offering rewards of £10,000 for information leading to the convictions of persons involved in the deaths of members of both the RIC and the Dublin Metropolitan Police. Rewards of £1,000 were also offered for 'secret' information about culprits, and free pardons offered to those involved in ambushes, provided that such persons were not the actual killers themselves.[52]

Following the death of Hunt, the killing of Wilson took priority for Commandant James Leahy, who described him as 'being on our black books because of his ruthless conduct in the treatment of Republicans'.[53] The IRA had already attempted to kill Wilson on 11 November 1918, the day that the Great War ended. Volunteer Edward McGrath went to Templemore with orders to shoot Wilson if the opportunity arose. Seeing Wilson, McGrath followed with the intention of shooting him, but abandoned the attempt as it was the first Armistice Day and the town was 'full of soldiers, many of them drunk, celebrating the cessation of hostilities in France. They had many civilian supporters and I considered that on that evening Templemore was no place for a lone armed IRA man.'[54] In June 1920 Wilson had another narrow escape when his head was grazed by bullets fired at an RIC patrol as they passed through the village of Templetouhy, and he must have known that he was a marked man following the murder of Michael Hunt in Thurles. Newspapers subsequently reported that 'he had a premonition of death and took great precautions', sometimes staying in the RIC barracks, and his house 'Manna Cottage' was periodically guarded by the RIC.[55]

The death of IRA member Captain Michael Small from Borrisoleigh on the night of 3 July 1920 sealed Wilson's fate. An IRA party had lain in wait for several hours to attack Shevry RIC barracks, but a military convoy from Templemore arrived unexpectedly, forcing the attack to be abandoned. Small asked Commandant Leahy for permission to return to his home in Upperchurch to attend confession and tend to his cattle, but as he was travelling across fields he was spotted by a joint RIC and military patrol, which opened fire, fatally wounding him. His body was removed to the mortuary at Richmond Barracks. During the subsequent inquest, medical evidence was given that Small had been shot several times, including once in the head at close range. Leahy attended the inquest and believed from the evidence given that Wilson, who had been in command of the patrol, had ordered the firing to begin and was therefore directly responsible for the death of Small. Leahy discussed the issue with other brigade officers and the decision was taken to shoot Wilson 'at any cost and as soon as possible'.[56] On 14 August 1920, a number of IRA Volunteers spent the day in Templemore with the intention of killing Wilson if the opportunity arose, but they did not see him.[57]

Returning to the town on 16 August, an IRA party consisting of Commandants Paddy Kinnane and Jimmy Leahy and Volunteers 'big' Jim Stapleton, John Fahy and Jack Ryan spent several hours lying in wait. At about 6.45 p.m. Wilson was seen leaving the RIC barracks and walking towards the nearby post office, dressed in plain clothes. As Wilson was about to enter the post office he was shot once in the head from the adjoining laneway by Jim Stapleton, who had also been responsible for killing DI Hunt.[58] Local general practitioner Doctor Mitchell was passing the scene and attended to Wilson, who was carried into Percy's grocery shop in George Street, but the district inspector was already dead. The following day the letters which Wilson had been carrying when he walked to the post office were returned to his family at Manna Cottage, still stained with his blood. They were invitations to the wedding of his daughter, which had been due to take place a few weeks later. The IRA party hurriedly left the area and used back roads to get to a safe house in the nearby village of Barnane. It was reported that a motor car carrying unknown men was seen 'rushing from the town at a furious speed'.[59]

Wilson was described by newspapers as a man of 'giant stature, well known in Tipperary', who had taken charge of Thurles RIC district as well as his own district of Templemore following the murder of DI Hunt several months earlier.[60] Reporting the murder to Dublin Castle, County Inspector Dunlop said that 'Wilson's fearless manner in dealing with Sinn Féin was the cause of his death'. He went on to say that the 'whole efforts of the Sinn Féin party are directed against the police and everything conceivable is being done to make their lives unbearable'.[61] Dunlop also said that even though the murder took place in broad daylight, 'no assistance to the identity of the men involved has been forthcoming'.[62] An inquest, held on 17 August at Richmond Barracks, collapsed as only six of the nineteen jurors summoned attended because of intimidation, resulting in fines for those who had absented themselves.[63]

The funeral service for William Harding Wilson took place at St Mary's Church of Ireland in Templemore on 19 August, and he was buried in the adjacent cemetery. Full military honours were provided by the Northamptonshire Regiment, garrisoned at Richmond. General Hugh Tudor, Chief of Police for Ireland, and RIC Inspector General Thomas J. Smyth attended. Methodist minister Reverend W.T. Cairns, a friend of the family and one of three minsters who conducted the funeral service, subsequently wrote to the family saying that William could have retired from the RIC but 'chose to play the manlier part and remain at his post in the hour of his country's need'. He also said that as William 'lay in his coffin with the red scars on his brow, he looked nobler in death than in life'.[64] Wilson left behind a widow, Frances, as well as sons Eccles George and Wesley H. and daughter Margery.[65] His headstone carries the epitaph 'his life for Ireland, his soul for God'. The local RIC ordered public houses in Templemore to remain closed during the funeral 'to avoid any excuse for further outbreaks'.[66] Mrs Frances Wilson subsequently received compensation to the amount of £20,000 for the death of her husband.[67]

In August 1919, when the 1st Battalion of the Northamptonshire Regiment arrived in Templemore from Northampton under the command of Lieutenant Colonel H.R.H. Drew, DSO (Distinguished Service

Order), they were not to know that they would be the last contingent of the British Army ever to serve in Richmond Barracks. By coincidence, the same regiment had also been the first to serve in Templemore when its predecessor, the 48th Foot, arrived in December 1814.[68] The Northamptonshire Regiment formed part of the 18th Brigade of the 6th Division, headquartered in Limerick. The division also included the 2nd Green Howards, 2nd Royal Welch Fusiliers, 1st Oxfordshire and Buckinghamshire Light Infantry and 2nd Royal Scots. The area of operations for the brigade were the counties of Limerick, Clare and North Tipperary.[69]

Upon arrival in Templemore, the 1st Battalion was engaged on duties which included 'organised drives across country, searches for arms and wanted rebels, patrols to maintain communications and assistance to the local constabulary'.[70] On the night of Wilson's death, 'wild scenes were witnessed' as reprisals took place in Templemore and surrounding areas. The *Tipperary Star* reported that soldiers joined in the outbreak: volleys were fired along the streets, several houses were attacked and one shop was looted.[71] The town hall in Templemore was burned to the ground, and creameries at Castleiney, Loughmore and Killea destroyed.[72] Creameries were a popular target for reprisals by the police and military as their destruction caused disproportionate hardship for a rural population primarily dependent on agriculture. Over 100 Irish creameries were destroyed between 1919 and 1922.[73]

The destruction of the town hall resulted in the deaths of two soldiers of the Northamptonshire Regiment, Captain Sidney Herbert Beattie, MC (Military Cross), and Lance Corporal Herbert John Fuggle. Workmen found 'a quantity of bones and a twisted bayonet' when clearing the ruins of the town hall after the fire.[74] The scene was cordoned off by soldiers and local general practitioner Doctor Mitchell invited to inspect the bones. When he concluded that the remains were human, they were removed to the mortuary in Richmond Barracks.[75] Fuggle, from Market Harborough in Leicestershire, was just 18 years of age. The death of Captain Beattie generated much publicity as he belonged to a prominent Dublin family, the fourth son of Sir Andrew Beattie and Lady Beattie of 46 Fitzwilliam Square West.[76] Sir Andrew was a former Lord Mayor and Deputy Lord Lieutenant of Dublin, and a serving member of Dublin Corporation. Sidney Beattie was born in Dublin on 10 May 1888 and educated at St Andrew's College. He was commissioned as a lieutenant in the Northamptonshire Regiment in 1912. Two of his brothers, Major A. Ernest Beattie and Captain J. Osborne Beattie, were also career army officers.

Beattie had been wounded three times during the Great War, receiving a shrapnel wound at the Battle of Neuve Chapelle in 1915, a gunshot wound to the left arm at the Battle of Fleurs in 1916 and another shrapnel wound during the Battle of Messines in 1917. He reached the rank of lieutenant colonel during the war, but reverted to his former rank of captain when the army reduced in size following the cessation of hostilities in 1918. Beattie had been awarded the MC in 1917, the citation commending his conspicuous gallantry and devotion to duty: 'by his personal coolness, initiative and resource, supervised the work under fire, remaining at his post although wounded, and setting a splendid example of what an officer's conduct should be at all times, especially in an emergency.'[77]

Beattie was posted to Russia in May 1919 with the 'Slavo-British Legion' before rejoining his regiment in Templemore during October 1919. Reporting the deaths to the War Office in London, Major E.L. Hughes indicated that Beattie 'of the battalion under my command died at 0630 today in the military hospital, Tipperary as the result of injuries caused by a fall from a burning building in the town of Templemore on the night of 16th/17th August 1920'. The regimental diary stated that Beattie 'died of accidental injuries' and that Fuggle had 'accidentally burnt to death'.[78]

The *Irish Times* reported that Beattie, with complete disregard for his own safety, had entered the burning town hall to rescue a trapped civilian.[79] The *Northampton Daily Chronicle* stated that Beattie had died heroically 'attempting to rescue a man from a fire'.[80] The *Tipperary Star* gave a different version of events, however, reporting that the military had taken petrol at gunpoint from Moynan's garage, and when the town hall was set ablaze a cheer was given and a voice shouted 'Sinn Féiners all lie down'.[81] George Moynan stated that a number of policemen entered his shop, threatened him and his staff with revolvers and then, taking cans of petrol, smashed windows and set fire to the premises. Moynan went on to say that he did not know why he was targeted as he had been on 'very friendly terms with District Inspector Wilson'.[82] The IRA Volunteers responsible for killing Wilson saw the town hall in Templemore ablaze from their hiding place on the slopes of the Devil's Bit Mountain near the village of Barnane.[83]

The following day, Volunteer James Duggan visited Templemore and later described the 'gruesome spectacle' of the town hall in ashes and the streets strewn with broken glass and debris.[84] Some efforts were made by the police to curb the excesses of the military, with one newspaper reporting that the actions of 'RIC sergeants Paden and Begley in restraining the military in their work of destruction is favourably commented on'.[85]

Sir Andrew Beattie was also a member of Dublin Corporation, and the death of his son led to the passing of a resolution of sympathy by the Corporation. Richard Mulcahy, chief of staff of the IRA, was a member of the Sinn Féin group which controlled the Corporation. When news of the resolution reached Tipperary, it 'dumbfounded' local Volunteers.[86]

Commandant Jimmy Leahy sent a strongly worded letter of protest to Mulcahy 'blaming him in particular for having made no attempt to find out the facts before agreeing to the resolution of sympathy.'[87] Leahy heard no more about the matter, but subsequently believed that Mulcahy did not like him, even though they once had been on friendly terms. Personal antipathies and internecine feuding within the IRA frequently led to tense relationships between GHQ and local commanders.[88] Dan Breen threatened to resign over the issue, but a letter intercepted by British military intelligence from the HQ of the 3rd Tipperary Brigade shows the response which Breen received to this threat:

> Re yours to the chief of staff – for God's sake Dan, have a bit of sense. What the hell do you or I need to care about the Dublin Corporation? Besides Dan, the evidence that Beattie was there to burn the town hall would not hang a cat in any court of justice.[89]

The letter went on to say that the issue was not serious enough to warrant the resignation of Mulcahy and other IRA members from Dublin Corporation. Breen was asked to reconsider his threat to resign over the matter, and his suggestion that an IRA contingent from Tipperary should travel across the Irish Sea to 'burn England' was also referred to, but the writer stated that 'IRA GHQ were reluctant to do so'.[90] Prior to the destruction of Templemore town hall, the relationship between Mulcahy and the Tipperary IRA had already been difficult, as the Soloheadbeg ambush had been carried out against his express orders as IRA chief of staff. Mulcahy believed, however, that insofar as the Tipperary men were concerned, 'their services were not required and their presence was often awkward' in Dublin.[91]

Concluding his monthly report to Dublin Castle for August 1920, the RIC Inspector General referred to the bitterness of feeling displayed in Munster and the commitment of the IRA to break the morale of the police. He reported his belief that the IRA viewed the police as 'the last obstacle in the way of the establishment of an Irish Republic'.[92] Printed notices were posted in several counties denouncing the police as spies and traitors, and warning persons not to speak to them or in any way tolerate their existence under penalty of death. As the guerrilla war in Tipperary escalated, the military found innovative ways to respond. For example, the IRA regularly blocked roads by digging trenches and felling trees prior to staging an ambush or to disrupt the movement of military and police convoys.

In Templemore this tactic was countered when soldiers forced local residents to saw the felled trees at gunpoint and deliver them to Richmond Barracks, and then carry out repairs to the roads. The regimental diary cynically noted that while 'the innocent may have suffered for the guilty, it was noticeable that tree-felling rapidly became less popular'.[93] A military inquiry into the damage caused by the reprisal of 20 August opened at Richmond Barracks on 25 August, at which the owners of affected property gave evidence. They were represented by solicitors, but the public were not admitted.[94] In total, compensation claims totalling £184,000 were lodged with North Tipperary County Council in respect of the burnings and other damage. As the conflict intensified it became almost a matter of routine that attacks on the police and military were met with an almost instantaneous response involving the burning of public buildings, shops and factories and damage to the property of actual or suspected members of Sinn Féin or the IRA.

On 21 August 1920, the 'Restoration of Order in Ireland Act' (ROIA) came into effect. Stopping short of the powers which would be given to the military if full martial law were introduced, the ROIA provided for the suspension of trial by jury in favour of military courts-martial. Intended for use in the most disturbed counties where the king's writ had effectively ceased to function, the new legislation did not produce the desired effect for the government and martial law was introduced in counties Cork, Kerry, Limerick and Tipperary on 9 December 1920. The death of District Inspector William Wilson and the reprisal attacks which followed triggered the surreal series of events which achieved international fame and became known as the period of the 'Templemore Miracles'.

VISIONARIES: 'SUPERNATURAL MANIFESTATIONS, ACCOMPANIED BY CURES'[1]

Immediately after the deaths of Beattie and Fuggle during the burning of Templemore town hall on 16 August, the first reports of 'supernatural manifestations accompanied by cures' occurring in the area appeared in local and national newspapers.[2] Attention was focused on a shop at Main Street in Templemore and a cottage in the townland of Curraheen near the village of Gortagarry, 12km from Templemore. It was reported that religious statues in the shop of merchant and newsagent Thomas Dwan in Main Street, Templemore, the nearby Royal Irish Constabulary barracks and the cottage of Thomas Dwan's sister-in-law, Miss Maher, at Curraheen were shedding tears of blood. It was also reported that 16-year-old James Walsh, known to all as Jimmy, who was employed as a farm labourer by Miss Maher and also lived in the cottage, was experiencing Marian apparitions, and that a 'holy well' had appeared in the floor of his bedroom.

Thomas Dwan, described by Hugh Martin, special correspondent of the *Daily News*, as a 'fat, bull-necked man with a heavy moustache and small eyes', was interviewed at length by reporters.[3] He told them that strange occurrences had been taking place both in his home and in the Curraheen cottage for several weeks. Following the murder of District Inspector Wilson he had a 'premonition that he was to be the medium of making them known publically'.[4] Dwan claimed that the Blessed Virgin appeared to Jimmy Walsh in his presence, but while she spoke to Walsh, he could not hear what she had said. Immediately after this, 'all of the statues in my house and in the house in Curraheen began bleeding'.[5] Miss Maher was interviewed and claimed that several weeks earlier, while Jimmy Walsh was returning from the local creamery, the Virgin Mary appeared to him in the form of a nun. Miss Maher also claimed that the apparition had returned on several occasions since then, and was 'visible to young children … although I could not see it'.[6] The *Tipperary Star* reported that after the burning of Templemore town hall, 'some of the statues from which blood had been oozing were taken by Walsh to Templemore from the cottage in Curraheen […] It was believed by many local people that this action had saved the town from destruction'.[7] The *Limerick Leader* described how prominent townsmen had gathered around the bleeding statues to pray, 'thanking God that the town was saved, and that none of the inoffensive people of Templemore suffered any casualties'.[8] As the military had sworn to sack the town and 'make the Catholics pay for it' following the deaths of District Inspector Wilson, Captain Beattie and Lance Corporal Fuggle, some people believed that divine intervention had taken place to prevent the town being destroyed in revenge, and that 'our Lady had saved Templemore'.[9] On 31 August 1920, County Inspector Dunlop of the Royal Irish Constabulary in Nenagh reported to the inspector general at Dublin Castle:

On 20th inst. miraculous apparitions are alleged to have appeared in Templemore and Curraheen. Sacred statues belonging to a man named Walsh and a constable stationed at Templemore are alleged to have begun to bleed, and several miraculous cures are said to have taken place.[10]

Constable Thomas Wimsey was the policeman referred to. It was reported that a religious statue had been given to Wimsey by Walsh several weeks earlier, and had been kept in the dormitory he shared in the barracks.[11] Dunlop had this statue removed and placed with other statues on an improvised altar placed in the yard beside Dwan's shop. This followed an incident during which the barracks was besieged by hundreds of pilgrims pleading to see and touch the statue. Some managed to gain entry to the premises and had to be forcibly removed by the police.[12] When reporters asked to interview Wimsey, they were informed that he was 'seriously ill and could not be seen'.[13] One newspaper reported that Constable Wimsey was planning to leave the RIC and join a religious order.[14] Wimsey, who had twenty-seven years' service in the force, resigned on 7 September 1920 with 'no reason given'.[15]

As the conflict intensified, police morale deteriorated rapidly and the number of resignations increased from an average of eleven per week in January 1920 to fifty-two per week by June that year.[16] Reasons given for resignations varied, with some men stating that they left because of intimidation or fear, while others responded to pressure from family or friends. Other policemen cited ethical or moral reasons for their resignations. The campaign of intimidation against potential applicants ensured that many Irishmen were reluctant to join the police, leading to the creation of two separate and distinct organisations: the Royal Irish Constabulary Special Reserve, colloquially known as the 'Black and Tans', and the Auxiliary Division, Royal Irish Constabulary (ADRIC). While the Black and Tans were part of the regular RIC the Auxiliary Division, known as 'temporary cadets', consisted primarily of former military officers and operated in companies of 100 with their own command structures, acting independently of local police and the military. The arrival of these reinforcements in Ireland had a disastrous impact on relations between the police and the people, especially in counties such as Tipperary where violence was prevalent.

The vacated mansion of Sir John Carden at Templemore Abbey was occupied by B Company of ADRIC, the only company stationed in Tipperary, and which combined with G Company from Killaloe in County Clare for operations in northern Tipperary. South Tipperary was the responsibility of auxiliary companies based in Kilkenny and north Cork. A temporary shortage of complete RIC uniforms led to the new arrivals being temporarily issued with a mixture of army and police clothing, which resulted in the application of the epithet Black and Tans. The appearance of these new policemen generated much interest, with the *Tipperary Star* reporting that police attired in 'khaki uniform, but wearing police caps arrived at Nenagh railway station … their mixed uniform attracted a considerable amount of attention as they marched to barracks'.[17]

The journal of the Volunteers, *An t-Óglách*, quickly denounced the new arrivals as 'physically and morally degenerate Englishmen' and asserted that the IRA would 'make short work of them'.[18] While IRA propaganda portrayed the Black and Tans and Auxiliaries as reprobates, categorising them among other things as the 'sweepings of English gaols', many were in fact decorated veterans of the 1914–18 war. Of the 2,200 men who served in the Auxiliary Division, 633 held gallantry awards, including three with the Victoria Cross (VC), twenty-two with the Distinguished Service Order (DSO), 135 with the MC and twenty-three with the Distinguished Conduct Medal (DCM). In parallel with the deployment of the new police reinforcements in Ireland, General Sir Neville Macready, former Commissioner of the London Metropolitan Police, was appointed commander-in-chief of all crown forces in Ireland. The press reported that he had been given practically a free hand by the Cabinet to suppress the rebellion by whatever means may be requisite.[19] The Black and Tans and Auxiliary Division soon acquired reputations for brutality and indiscipline. William O'Brien, a former Member of Parliament, described them as 'desperadoes of the vilest type'.[20]

For many Irish-born policemen with long service, the reinforcements were a 'revelation, a plague and a Godsend … they brought help but they frightened even those that they had come to help'.[21] Sergeant Shea of the RIC in Templemore wrote to his family in the province of Ulster telling them that the newcomers had:

> neither religion or morals, used foul language, had the old soldier's talent for dodging and scrounging, spoke in strange accents, called the Irish natives, associated with low company, stole from one another, sneered at the customs of the country, drank to excess and put sugar on their porridge.[22]

In June 1920 a formal boycott of the police and all associated with them had been issued by IRA headquarters. The inspector general of the RIC informed the British government of his concerns about 'how much longer the force could withstand such strain'.[23] As news of the alleged miracles and cures in Templemore spread, it was estimated that upwards of 15,000 people per day were making the pilgrimage to the town and then on to the cottage at Curraheen. The flood of pilgrims brought substantial economic benefits to the area, which one newspaper stated 'must have done better than many a seaside town in Ireland this year'.[24] County Inspector Dunlop stated to Dublin Castle that the alleged miracles were having a positive effect on the locality, describing the conduct of the large crowds as 'exemplary'.[25] Apart from the RIC barracks, it was also reported that when Jimmy Walsh visited Grey's boot-makers shop in Georges Street in the company of three Roman Catholic priests, a statue 'wept copiously in their presence'.[26] That statue was subsequently moved to the improvised grotto which had been set up in a yard at the side of Thomas Dwan's shop in the main street of Templemore. Walsh claimed that he had been approached by a British soldier who claimed to have seen a 'beautiful lady near the town hall ruins … she said come to me and you will be saved'.[27] Templemore was now referred to as 'Pilgrimville' or 'Pilgrimstown' by some newspapers, although a sceptical local who wrote articles for the *Tipperary Star* under the pseudonym of 'Dr Mick' instead referred to Templemore as the 'town of the home-made miracles'.[28] To cater for the thousands of visitors categorised by one reporter as 'the halt, the maim and the blind', extra trains from Kingsbridge (now Heuston) station in Dublin were added to the normal schedule.[29]

One of the first to visit Dwan's yard to view the statues was 7-year-old William O'Meara from Castleiney near Templemore, who was brought there by his brother. A table or improvised altar had been placed in the yard with a crucifix and several statues on it, and Mrs Dwan was holding aloft a statue of the Virgin Mary. O'Meara recalled seeing 'two streaks of blood' from the statue and that the 'whole town was crowded in around it gazing in wonderment'.[30] Reverend Collier, a correspondent for the *Catholic Times*, visited Templemore on 23 August and wrote that his train from Dublin was packed with pilgrims. He estimated that 6,000–8,000 people were outside Dwan's house, with many having been there overnight. Collier saw four statues, some with blood trickling down the face, neck, breasts or body.[31] Events in Templemore rapidly gained international attention, with the *New York Times* reporting that 'crowds of awed people witnessed the strange manifestation and wonderful cures are being effected'.[32]

Hugh Martin of the *Daily News* wrote that he saw Thomas Dwan open a ground-floor window in his house by a few inches, thus allowing visitors, many who had slept in the street the previous night, to see the statues. Scores of pilgrims dropped to their knees, heads were covered and rosary beads produced. The crowd grew steadily and by the early afternoon thousands were in the square, including 'paralysed children, old men with the palsy and lads with withered limbs … there was every deformity from warts to a club foot and almost every chronic malady from fainting fits to consumption'.[33] He went on to say that, 'An atmosphere charged with passion has been changed for one permeated with peace and pulsating with piety.'[34]

Thomas Dwan would lean out of the window and call out the names of people, who would be 'led, dragged or carried' into the yard and then into the presence of Jimmy Walsh.[35] Pilgrims who had spent long periods waiting in the main square to pray in front of the statues took pieces of gravel away as souvenirs or relics.[36] A shawl said to have belonged to Jimmy Walsh's mother was cut into pieces and sold as relics. On one occasion when Jimmy Walsh dismounted from his bicycle, pilgrims were seen to kiss the saddle of his bicycle, keen to have any contact, however tenuous, with the boy now referred to by newspapers as 'Saint Walsh'. Tipperary County Council erected railings in the square in an attempt to control the huge numbers of visitors, which included a number of priests and nuns visiting from the United States.[37] The *Daily Mirror* reported that, 'Sinn Féin volunteers armed with heavy sticks made vain attempts to preserve order, but the crowd could not restrain itself … women fainted by the score in the struggle.'[38]

Pilgrims were admitted to the shrine in batches of fifty, and after they had prayed for several minutes an IRA officer with 'watch in hand shouted time please … and another batch of pilgrims were admitted'.[39] The Dwan family and Jimmy Walsh were likened to 'besieged prisoners' because of the enormous crowds which surrounded the house. Special arrangements were made for those who could not walk, with 'invalids being carried to the shrine on the shoulders of volunteers'.[40]

One reporter expressed his surprise that few of the pilgrims seemed interested in viewing the ruins of the town hall which had been destroyed only a few days earlier and had resulted in the deaths of two men. He wrote that the damage had been done by 'government incendiarists … its charred, roofless wall and gaping windows, its smouldering debris made this building for me the object of curiosity and a symbol of frightfulness'. [41] When people arrived in front of the improvised altar 'with bated breath and reverent steps', they saw crudely written notices by Jimmy Walsh giving them instructions on what prayers should be offered. This consisted of a 'novena of seven Our Fathers and seven Hail Marys, in honour of tears shed at the foot of the cross'.[42]

Described by one newspaper as a 'saint if ever there was one', Jimmy Walsh told reporters that he had joined the Cistercian monastery in Roscrea as a novice, but had been forced to leave because of ill-health.[43] There are no records in the Cistercian monastery showing that Walsh was ever a novice in the order or had any connection with the monastery. Walsh told journalists that he had first started to experience Marian apparitions on 14 August 1920, and that religious statues in his bedroom began to move and shed tears of blood. He also said that the Virgin Mary had appeared to him in the form of a nun, and that her message was to 'convince the words against sin and pride … the miracle of Lourdes is to be repeated in Ireland'.[44] Walsh was not known to the local police nor to have had any involvement with the Irish Volunteers or Irish Republican Army, but his brother was arrested and imprisoned without charge or trial in London, where he had taken part in a hunger strike, along with many other Republican prisoners.[45]

Jimmy's father, Daniel Walsh, a labourer, married Mary Mulcahy in Holycross church on 26 September 1893, and their first child, John, was born four months later in January 1894 at Newtown. The couple moved frequently around the Thurles area and lived at various times in Ballinahow, Beakstown, Bouladuff and Dovea, where Jimmy was born in 1904. Daniel and Mary Walsh had a total of twelve children as follows: John (born 11 January 1894), Patrick (12 April 1895), Mary (8 September 1896), Daniel (8 November 1897), Sarah (19 July 1899), Honoria (6 January 1901), Bridget (6 January 1903), James (16 February 1904), Mary (20 July 1905), Kieren (6 June 1908), William (8 January 1910) and Martin (15 June 1911).

Jimmy told reporters that his intention was 'to join a religious order by entering the novitiate' of the De La Salle Order.[46] The 'simple-mannered youth', as he was referred to by one newspaper, quickly achieved fame not only in Ireland but also internationally.[47] Within days, advertising had appeared in local and national newspapers offering for sale 'photographs of the boy to whom the blessed virgin appeared' as well as a myriad of religious souvenirs.[48]

Most pilgrims who visited Templemore then travelled on to the cottage at Curraheen, which was equally regarded as a place of pilgrimage because of the reported existence of a holy well in the floor of Walsh's bedroom.[49] Miss Maher told reporters that Walsh, acting on instructions from the apparition, had dug a heart-shaped hole in his bedroom floor from which a 'holy well appeared ... producing a great volume of water'.[50] She claimed that she had seen all of the religious statues in the cottage 'alight of their own accord around the little spring'. Walsh 'fell prostrate ... and the apparition said "fear not", before vanishing'.[51] The practice of pilgrimage to holy wells predates the introduction of Christianity to Ireland, but in more recent times had been closely linked with Marian devotion. Pilgrims to the well at Curraheen adhered to the traditional practice of reciting five decades of the rosary before kneeling beside the well and praying. They then walked three times around the well before drinking from it, and also took water to bring home.[52]

The huge number of pilgrims visiting the area prompted one elderly local to make an analogy with the Alaskan gold rush of 1897–98 that he had personally experienced, saying that it had been 'easier to get from Skagway to the Klondike than from Templemore to Curraheen ... another Dawson City had arisen, a city of tents and shacks'.[53] As in Templemore, souvenirs were highly prized and 'pieces of stone and clay were carefully packed and carried away as things of priceless value'.[54] Hugh Martin of the *Daily News* visited the cottage and wrote that, 'poor wretches long past help were dragged through boreens to their inevitable disappointment ... the picture of one young woman staggering upwards with her tortured child will be long in leaving me'.[55]

As rumours of apparitions and miracles spread, the number of pilgrims visiting Templemore rose significantly. Tents appeared in the main square, with one reporter comparing it to 'an early settlement in the Australian bush'. Marquees were set up by travelling traders and were also made available to pilgrims at night for use as accommodation. Some pilgrims who could not afford to pay slept in the 'shelter afforded by carts'.[56] Vehicles from all over Ireland came to the town, as evidenced by the variety of county registration plates noted by reporters. Hotels, guesthouses and every form of accommodation in the locality were 'besieged' by travellers returning from Templemore, and food and other supplies were in short supply.[57] One newspaper described the 'lodgings and hotel accommodation insufficient for even a fourth of the visitors, and the town's food stocks are virtually exhausted'. It was further said that neighbouring towns and villages were 'overflowing with people'.[58] A tea room was opened at Jail Street in Templemore by charitable townspeople to help feed 'poorer pilgrims who could not afford hotel prices'.[59]

Mrs Muriel Cambie of the White House in Templemore, wife of Templemore general practitioner Doctor Edward Cambie, wrote to the *Tipperary Star* newspaper appealing for people to provide accommodation and food to 'sleep and feed the masses'. She stated that, 'Prices in the tea room are low to the poor … but to those who can afford more we charge more, which is gladly paid.'[60] Mrs Cambie knew Jimmy Walsh personally and put pen to paper defending him against those who doubted his bona fides. She described him as a 'saintly boy … a humble lad with neither the education or gilded surroundings to make him adept at deception and craft, nor has he lived the years to acquire them'.[61]

Some newspapers reported that many people had been cured or healed either by direct contact with Walsh or by exposure to the bleeding statues. Some visitors, however, were not convinced of the veracity of the apparitions. One journalist who visited Templemore and Curraheen wrote that he came 'to see a miracle and saw one … it was not a miracle of bleeding statues but of pathetic belief'.[62] He went on to say that he had viewed many 'sad spectacles of human suffering … the saddest of all was surely that of an imbecile lad of thirteen, brought forty miles by a distracted mother'.[63]

Newspapers including the *Limerick Leader* reported the case of former soldier Martin Monahan, the first person to personally claim that he had been cured.[64] Monahan had been in the Royal Irish Rifles and was medically discharged in 1918 after being badly wounded in the legs by shrapnel during the Battle of the Somme in 1916. After returning home he had spent a long period convalescing in the military hospital attached to Richmond Barracks. After the killing of District Inspector Wilson and reprisal which followed,

Monahan was readmitted to the hospital suffering from shell shock, or what is now known as post-traumatic stress disorder (PTSD). Monahan told reporters that after the news of the alleged cures and miracles taking place in the town reached him, he had 'crawled across the road' to Dwan's house. Walsh brought him upstairs and rubbed a crucifix on his wounded leg before praying with him and then asking him to say 'seven Our Fathers and seven Hail Marys in honour of the precious blood trickling from the cross'.[65] Monahan claimed that his pain had gone immediately, and he had been able to walk unaided from Dwan's house. Local curate Reverend John O'Neill commented that knowing Monahan, he was satisfied that the cure affected on him was genuine.

Sergeant Shea of Templemore RIC wrote to his family in Ulster saying that Monahan was known to everybody in the town, 'dragging his twisted legs between wooden crutches'. After his visit to Walsh, however, Shea said that he saw Monahan 'leaping around like a circus tumbler in front of a laughing, weeping, praying, hysterical crowd'.[66] Shea went on to say that people set out from all over the country for Templemore, including 'stretcher cases, babes in arms, invalids in wheelchairs, the mentally ill, the blind, the deformed … and outside the little cottage at Curraheen the pile of discarded crutches got bigger'.[67]

As a local policeman, however, Shea was acutely aware that the extraordinary events which were taking place in his police district could be used by the IRA militarily. He wrote that, 'Men on the run were moved, the disposition of active service groups rearranged and new supplies of arms and ammunition distributed.'[68]

Hugh Martin of the *Daily News* interviewed Monahan and his wife and concluded that the cure effected on him was miraculous, but in his opinion it was a case of faith-healing oneself rather than divine intervention.[69] Martin also spoke to a harness-maker called Danny Egan, who claimed to have been cured of sciatica. Martin did note that many of the reported cures related to 'nervous ailments, which are particularly susceptible to treatment by powerful suggestion'.[70] The *Irish Examiner* reported that a cancer sufferer who had returned to Cork from Templemore claimed that the pain in his afflicted parts had disappeared, and he was now able to take food with 'normal facility'.[71] Other well-publicised cases included those of a Ms Guerin and Mr Gavin from Limerick, who were allegedly cured of 'paralysis' and 'acute hip disease' respectively. It was also claimed that a Mrs Campion was cured of blindness and a Ms Helena Crowe cured of paralysis.[72] Reports of miraculous cures were not just confined to Templemore during this period, however. Alleged cures were reported at St Winifred's Well in Wales, and there were also 'notable cures' amongst a party of 500 pilgrims from England who had visited the grotto at Lourdes in France. One unexpected consequence of the religious fervour which gripped the Templemore area came to light when it was reported that Archbishop Harty had administered confirmation to seven English soldiers, 'converts to Roman Catholicism … they were stationed in Templemore and were impressed by the apparitions in that town'.[73]

The word 'miracle' has been defined as 'an extraordinary event taken to manifest the supernatural power of God fulfilling his purpose'.[74] The Anglican writer C.S. Lewis defined the phenomenon as 'an interference with nature by supernatural powers'.[75] In 1730 Cardinal Prospero Lambertini, who later became Pope Benedict XIV, wrote an encyclical which specified the procedure to be followed when investigating whether extraordinary events could only be attributed to divine intervention. Marian apparitions, for example, had to be experienced simultaneously by multiple witnesses for them to be considered. The cautious attitude adopted by the Roman Catholic Church towards events in Templemore was consistent with its normal procedure when investigating such claims. Following reported apparitions at Guadalupe, Mexico, in 1531 which were accepted as genuine, three centuries passed without other confirmed cases.

The nineteenth century brought a resurgence in reports of Marian apparitions, drawing large numbers of pilgrims to sites in France, including La Salette in 1848, Lourdes in 1858 and Pontmain in 1871. There were also reported Marian apparitions in Knock,

Ireland, in 1879, and Fatima, Portugal, in 1917. Knock was the last significant Marian apparition of the nineteenth century, but did not receive ecclesiastical recognition from the Roman Catholic Church until 1936. This followed two episcopal commissions which investigated the reported apparitions and associated cures and interviewed all fifteen visionaries, finding 'no fault with their credibility'.[76] Despite the reticence of the Church, the fame of Knock spread and the miracles and cures attributed to it enabled the practice of devotion to the Virgin Mary to thrive in Ireland.

Despite the influx of pilgrims and the reported cures in Templemore, the official position of the Roman Catholic Church towards events in Templemore and Curraheen remained one of 'extreme reserve'.[77] Dr Michael Fogarty, Bishop of Killaloe, cautioned mass-goers that there had been no authoritative declaration by the Roman Catholic Church on the reality of the alleged apparitions in Templemore and Curraheen, and that the facts were diligently being inquired into by the Church. He said that people 'should restrain their judgement and not allow themselves to be carried away by excitement or popular rumour'.[78] Reverend Kiely, parish priest of Templemore, refused to visit the statues on several occasions, saying that he did not wish to 'give any sanction whatever to it, the more opposition it meets the better it will be, for if genuine it will prove itself.'[79] In private correspondence he wrote, 'If the thing is a prank it will fizzle out, if not why should

I stop it?'[80] Another priest declared all of the people concerned with the miracles to be 'stark mad'.[81]

Jimmy Walsh began to travel to other towns in the company of members of the clergy, first visiting Mount Mellary Abbey in County Waterford and then the town of Cashel in south Tipperary, where he stayed overnight in the presbytery on 10 September 1920 as guest of parish priest Monsignor Innocent Ryan. Walsh was specifically invited to Cashel by Ryan so that he could be closely watched. It was believed by some clergy that Walsh had a technique of sucking blood from his gums and then placing it on the statues and crucifixes, so those items were placed in locked rooms to see if they would bleed without being in the presence of Walsh.[82] The *Irish Times* reported that statues and a crucifix in the presbytery in Cashel had begun to bleed when touched by Walsh.[83]

As news spread in the town that Walsh was visiting, 'a piteous and clamorous crowd of invalids' arrived at the presbytery demanding to see and touch the statues which were on public display outside the building.[84] Monsignor Ryan subsequently wrote to newspapers in an attempt to halt the flow of pilgrims to Cashel. He cautioned the public not to put their faith in statues or crucifixes, but in the sacraments, and requested editors to give him 'space to tell the public that there are no bleeding statues or crucifixes here for anyone to see'.[85] No cures were reported in Cashel during Walsh's visit, and Ryan expressed the opinion that further investigation into the events would 'quickly clear the air and make known the truth'.[86] He further wrote that he 'doubted it from the beginning, and I now disbelieve in it, this ought to satisfy for the present all pious inquirers'.[87] He also said that he had told Jimmy Walsh that he had no faith in the supernatural nature of the alleged apparitions and would have none until with his own eyes he 'saw them confirmed by a live miracle – the blind seeing; the dumb speaking or the deaf hearing'.[88]

Many members of the clergy visited Templemore at this time, including Patrick Clune, Archbishop of Perth in Western Australia. Clune became a key figure during the Anglo-Irish War, acting as an intermediary between Michael Collins and the government of Prime Minister Lloyd George. The ongoing contact between Clune and Collins caused Mark Sturgis, assistant secretary at Dublin Castle, to remark in frustration that, 'The Archbishop sees Collins apparently without difficulty in Dublin, yet our intelligence fails to find him after weeks of searching.'[89] During his stay in Templemore, Clune met local IRA commanders including Jimmy Leahy, but when Clune tried to leave the town he could not get out because of the large number of pilgrims. Clune asked the IRA for assistance and a car which had brought pilgrims from Galway to Templemore was commandeered. The driver was ordered to take Clune to Limerick, and on arrival the archbishop offered money to the driver, who refused to take it.

When questioned as to why he would not accept the payment, he replied, 'Sure wasn't I commandeered in the name of the Republic!'[90]

Despite the fact that many IRA men were devout Roman Catholics, there were ongoing tensions between the Church and the IRA as the conflict progressed. Some priests advocated excommunication of IRA Volunteers while others were actively involved with Sinn Féin or the IRA. On 27 December 1920, for example, Templemore curate Fr Hickey was arrested by the military and detained in Richmond Barracks over the Christmas period on suspicion that he had 'administered aid to a wounded man who had taken part in an ambush at Borrisoleigh'.[91] On 6 September 1920, Doctor Harty, Catholic Archbishop of the Diocese of Cashel and Emly, delivered a sermon during which he denounced the ongoing political violence, stating that 'every crime committed was a stain on the faith, and also on national honour'.[92] He also referred to his recent visit to Pope Benedict XV in Rome, who encouraged the people of Ireland while working for the glory and freedom of their country to always do so 'within the law of God'.[93]

Leahy visited Canon M.K. Ryan in Thurles and requested that the apparitions and cures be denounced from the pulpit, which might deter pilgrims from travelling to Templemore and Curraheen. Leahy did not receive a positive reception from Canon Ryan, who 'appeared unimpressed by what I said'.[94] When these surreal events had begun, IRA Volunteers were as intrigued as everyone else in the area at what was taking place. Many Volunteers were staunch Roman Catholics with a particular devotion to the Virgin Mary and also to the rosary. For example, on 2 June 1921 an ambush took place at Modreeney near Borrisokane in north Tipperary during which four RIC constables were killed. While the ambush was taking place, Paddy Kennedy, the IRA officer in command, was seen firing at the police with a shotgun while his rosary beads hung around his neck.[95]

Jimmy Leahy and other IRA commanders concluded that decisive action must be taken to halt the influx of pilgrims and bring the Templemore Miracles to an end. Leahy stated that most of the older clergy treated the whole affair with caution, but some younger priests appeared to look 'upon Curraheen as another Lourdes, and Walsh as a saint'.[96] Reporting the situation in Templemore to GHQ in Dublin, Vice Commandant Edward McGrath wrote that the town was packed with pilgrims, beggars, stall-holders and undesirables. The police and military had 'disappeared off the streets and the IRA had taken over. They controlled traffic, introduced parking and restored order.'[97] The Volunteers also went around the Templemore area 'commandeering butter, milk and other food to feed the pilgrims … payment was of course made'.[98] The local IRA requested assistance from the neighbouring 1st Tipperary Brigade.

An informal truce developed between opposing forces in the extraordinary circumstances which prevailed. Volunteers acted as stewards and marshals but did not appear in uniform, and some soldiers and policemen even joined the pilgrimage. The unofficial truce was not complete, however; for example, IRA member Michael Troy was arrested while directing pilgrim traffic and taken to Richmond Barracks for interrogation, and advantage was taken by the IRA of the absence of the military and police from the streets to carry out reconnaissance of potential targets and scout suitable locations for future ambushes.[99] Troy was subsequently released without charge after being detained for two weeks in Limerick Prison. No 'explanation or apology was given for his arrest and imprisonment'.[100] A considerable number of detainees were also kept in Richmond Barracks itself.[101]

On one occasion a party of four IRA men from the Limerick Brigade, led by Tomas O'Maoileoin, were trying to make their way home from Tipperary using back roads, but came upon a military checkpoint between Birdhill and Nenagh. As they were in a car stolen from the local RIC district inspector in Kilmallock, they decided to turn away from the checkpoint, causing the soldiers to open fire. The Volunteers opted to travel towards Templemore as 'there was a lot of traffic going that way and it would be a good thing to go with the general crowd'.[102] On arrival in the town, the Limerick men even got to see 'Saint Walsh' from a distance, and witnessed the Black and Tans raiding a house in the main street. In later life, O'Maoileoin recalled his amusement at the fact that the stolen car had not been recognised in Templemore, even though it had false number plates. The number used was DI 303, the DI standing for the district inspector that it had been stolen from, and 303 being the calibre of ammunition for Lee Enfield rifles which were used by both the British Army and the IRA. Again using the large crowds of pilgrims as cover, the Limerick Volunteers eventually made it safely back to the city.

A visitor to Templemore using the nom-de-plume 'Viator' (Latin for traveller) wrote of his experiences in a letter to the editor of the *Irish Catholic* newspaper. Starting at Maher's cottage at Curraheen, he noted the similarities between the hills, river and countryside and those of Lourdes, speculating that Jimmy Walsh may have wanted to establish a 'miraculous shrine amongst his native hills'. He described the well in Walsh's bedroom as 'the size of a man's hat, surrounded by eight small stones'.[103] He noted that in Lourdes the well never ran dry, but at Walsh's home pilgrims were not allowed to take water directly from the well itself but from a bucket in the kitchen. This was 'suspicious, as it would not at all be impossible to refill the bucket at night'.[104] As Viator travelled on to Templemore, he noted that the 'Sinn Féin Police' demanded payment as a toll to get into the town. Arriving at Dwan's yard where the statues were displayed, Thomas Dwan quizzed 'curious clergy and invalids about the diseases they suffered from' before allowing them access to the improvised shrine. Viator saw no blood on the statues but did see dried-in red liquid. Engaging in conversation with a priest who was also in the yard, Viator asked, 'What do you think of this business?' The priest replied that in his opinion it was 'the greatest fraud on earth'.[105] He also noted that the main square was packed with tents and motor cars from all parts of Ireland, and stalls were selling religious beads and other items 'at not too cheap a price'.[106] Dwan reacted angrily to the publication of this letter and wrote to the *Irish Catholic* refuting it, stating that the contents about the 'alleged bleeding statues were false in almost everything mentioned'.[107] He complained that the author 'had not the manliness nor honour to write his name or name the priest who had described events in Templemore as a fraud, whereas at least Rev Innocent Ryan had the courage of his convictions'.[108]

At the height of the fervour surrounding the Templemore Miracles, Commandant Leahy had imposed a charge of 2*s* 6*d* per day on all motor vehicles bringing pilgrims from Templemore to Curraheen. The tax was imposed to pay for repairs to roads which had been damaged by the throngs of pilgrims, and to pay the expenses of IRA Volunteers involved in traffic and crowd control duty. Work took place each night to prepare Templemore and the road to Curraheen for the crowds of pilgrims which would arrive the following day. One reporter wrote that, 'Pilgrimstown at night presents the appearance of a corporate city …

gangs of men assemble at midnight for the purpose of cleaning up after each day. Each street is thoroughly sprinkled with hoses and the damped dust is swept and carted away.'[109]

The imposition of the tax caused an outcry. Sinn Féin's Count T.D. O'Byrne, chairman of North Tipperary County Council met Leahy and other senior IRA commanders. O'Byrne pointed out that the charge was highly irregular. Leahy replied that 'everything had to be irregular to deal with the situation that had arisen'.[110] O'Byrne suggested that the council should take over the collection of the levy, but Leahy refused, saying that he intended to buy arms and ammunition with any balance left over after deducting the Volunteers' expenses.[111] This levy was in addition to the usual levies collected from the population by the IRA as they moved through the countryside, which were paid 'willingly and with good heart by the majority of the people'.[112]

Pilgrims were reported to be 'loud in their praise of the splendid men of Óglaig na hÉireann [the IRA] who maintained order and also prevented excessive profiteering by shopkeepers, caterers and hoteliers'.[113] Such profiteering was stringently dealt with by the IRA, who imposed a scale of charges after 'due enquiry, deliberation and consideration of the abnormal conditions prevailing'.[114] One newspaper report detailed the IRA court-martial of a driver from Cork who had charged pilgrims £6 instead of the normal 30*s* fare to transport them from Templemore to Curraheen.[115] Collection boxes on behalf of the IRA and Cumann na mBan (the League of Women, the women's auxiliary corps to the Irish Volunteers) were placed along the pilgrimage route, providing a substantial windfall for the brigade, with over £1,500 contributed by pilgrims.[116] Several weeks after the Templemore Miracles had begun, Leahy and other officers arranged a private interrogation of James Walsh. They had started to view the 'whole business with incredulity', and were also seriously concerned that volunteer discipline was being compromised.[117] Some pilgrims had begun to tip the IRA men, with the result that Volunteers who had been previously been abstemious and enthusiastic 'took to drink and began to forget that they were engaged in a life and death struggle for the country's freedom'.[118]

An IRA party led by Leahy interrogated Walsh in Dwan's house. Walsh told them that when he had questioned the apparition, the Virgin Mary had indicated her approval of the IRA campaign, including the shooting of policemen, and wished to see the campaign intensified. Leahy found it difficult 'to keep a straight face', concluding that Walsh was either 'mentally abnormal or a hypocrite.'[119] Leahy felt that the situation could not be allowed to continue, but was nonetheless not averse to profiting from it and demanded that Walsh donate to the IRA the money given to him by pilgrims. Walsh handed over £75 to Leahy and this money was subsequently passed to the brigade quartermaster. Following the meeting, the IRA determined that decisive action should be taken to halt the influx of pilgrims and bring the Templemore Miracles to an end. Leahy contacted Michael Collins to express his concern about the situation in Templemore and the detrimental effect it was having on volunteer discipline in the area. Collins issued an order that Walsh was to be brought to Dublin for interrogation.

When Walsh arrived in Dublin, Séamus Robinson, officer commanding the IRA's 3rd Tipperary Brigade, found to his irritation that 'the now notorious Walsh' had been brought to an IRA safe house at 71 Heytesbury Street which was used by Volunteers from Tipperary as a base in the capital. Dan Breen had brought Walsh to number 71 on the same day that IRA Volunteer Mick Lambe from Clonmel was 'brought and dumped there, badly wounded, semi-conscious, raving and bleeding profusely'. Dublin IRA Volunteers arranged for Lambe to be smuggled into the Mater Hospital to be treated in secret, but before he left, 'Breen arrived with Walsh hoping to get him to invoke his bleeding miracles'.[120] Robinson did not approve of Walsh's presence, believing that it might attract unwelcome attention. He later stated that it was 'no wonder Fernside followed soon after … and no wonder number 71 was raided for the first and second times immediately after'.[121]

What was dubbed the 'Battle of Fernside' by the IRA took place on 2 October 1920, when Dan Breen and Seán Treacy were hiding in a safe house at 37 Upper Drumcondra Road in Dublin. The house was owned by Professor Carolan, a lecturer in the nearby St Patrick's teacher-training college. The house was raided during the night by the police and military, and in the shootout that followed Carolan and two British officers were killed. Treacy and Breen escaped after shooting their way out. Breen was badly injured and was smuggled into the Mater hospital, where Mick Lambe was also being covertly treated. Treacy was also wounded, but not seriously.[122]

After leaving number 71, Walsh was taken to O'Neill's pub in Pearse Street, Dublin, which was owned by a Tipperary man and used by IRA Volunteers from the county who needed safe refuge in Dublin. Collins ordered Breen to interrogate 'this saint from Templemore … the fellow who operates the bleeding statue … Breen very reluctantly agreed to do.'[123] Neither Collins nor Breen were known for being overly religious; for example, when Collins made his maiden political speech in London in 1908 it was described as a 'violent attack upon the influence of the Catholic hierarchy and clergy'.[124] Breen recalled in later life that, 'we [Breen and Collins] did not trust Walsh … we thought he was a spy'.[125]

While Collins waited in the next room, Breen introduced himself to 'the saint' saying, 'How do you do boy?'. Walsh was only 16 years of age but was now under interrogation by Dan Breen, a wanted man with a fearsome reputation and a bounty of £1,000 on his head from the British government. Breen spoke to Walsh for about fifteen minutes and concluded that he 'was a fake'. Walsh was taken away and Breen returned to the room next door, where he spoke to Michael Collins about what had happened. Giving his opinion that the Templemore apparitions and miracles were not genuine, Collins derisively replied, 'One can't take any notice of what you say Breen, because you have no religion!'[126]

As Walsh was leaving O'Neill's public house, some IRA Volunteers who were there waiting to see Collins and Breen insisted on addressing him as 'saint' and kissing his coat. Commandant Dinny Lacey of the 3rd Tipperary Brigade spoke to Walsh and asked, 'The next time you meet the Blessed Virgin Mary, be sure to insist on nothing less than a republic.'[127] Tipperary IRA Volunteer Phil Shanahan, a veteran of the 1916 Rising who owned a pub in Dublin frequented by IRA members, was asked by Breen to drive Walsh back to Tipperary, and that was the last contact Breen had with the young man he described as 'the failure Walsh'.[128] Upon his return from Templemore, Shanahan offered Breen water from the holy well at Curraheen to drink, but Breen forcefully refused the offer. As doubts about the veracity of the miracles and cures attributed to them began to spread, and with Walsh having been taken away from Templemore, never to return, the IRA decided to take full control of the situation and resume the war in earnest, with deadly consequences.

Doris Ada Hill on her wedding day, 21 September 1932. (Courtesy of Rod Kippax)

Discarded crutches at Maher's house, Curraheen Cottage, September 1920. (Courtesy of the Garda College Museum)

IRA Volunteers guarding the improvised altar at Dwan's yard, September 1920. (Hogan collection, National Library of Ireland)

James and Doris Walsh with their daughter Isobel, Sydney 1932. (Courtesy of Rod Kippax)

Jimmy Walsh in Australia, 1920s. (Courtesy of Rod Kippax)

Jimmy Walsh, August 1920. (Courtesy of Peter Dwan)

Miss Maher's cottage at Currheen, where Jimmy Walsh lived, September 1920. (Courtesy of the Garda College Museum)

Mrs Dwan with statues, August 1920. (RTE Stills Library, ref. 0510.032)

People in front of the Bleeding Statues, 22 August 1920. Note the IRA Volunteers on either side of the arch. Photograph by W. D. Hogan. (Courtesy of the National Library of Ireland, HOG214)

Pilgrims outside Templemore RIC Barracks, August 1920. (Courtesy of Peter Dwan)

Pilgrims praying in Dwan's yard, August 1920. (RTE Stills Library, ref. 0510.030)

Mr and Mrs Thomas Dwan with statues, August 1920. (RTE Stills Library, ref. 0510.033)

Ruins of Templemore Town Hall, 17 August 1920. (Courtesy of the Garda College Museum)

Ruins of Templemore Town Hall and the surrounding streets, 17 August 1920. (Courtesy of the Garda College Museum)

Thomas Dwan and family, August 1920. (Courtesy of Peter Dwan)

AFTERMATH: 'A SECOND 'LOURDES!'[1]

The Royal Irish Constabulary barracks at Golding's Cross near Barnane village was on the pilgrimage route between Templemore and Curraheen, so was passed by thousands of pilgrims each day. On 29 September 1920, IRA Volunteers under the command of Jim Stapleton, the man who had killed both District Inspectors Hunt and Wilson, led an ambush on an RIC patrol as they returned to their barracks. Constable Edward Noonan, a Black and Tan from London, and Constable Terence Flood from Leitrim were 'riddled with bullets' and died instantly.[2] Constables Marnane and Ferris were wounded but managed to return fire before escaping. The IRA stopped a car containing pilgrims travelling from Curraheen to Templemore and ordered them to go to Richmond Barracks in Templemore with the 'dead bodies of the two policemen thrown across their knees in the car'.[3] Commenting on the effect of such reprisals on the civilian population, the RIC county inspector expressed his opinion that when the IRA committed an outrage such as the Kiloskehan ambush, 'no steps are taken to protect the locality from the consequences'.[4]

As the IRA had intended, the ambush brought a substantial number of military and police reinforcements into the area, who 'indulged in a reign of terror by indulging in indiscriminate firing into houses and across fields'.[5] Soldiers of the Northamptonshire Regiment visited the 'holy well' at Curraheen and also went to Dwan's yard in Templemore, where they removed crutches and other items which had been discarded by pilgrims. Some soldiers decorated themselves with religious artefacts, others feigned lameness while using the crutches, parading around the streets in mockery of the miracles. Rumours spread that Templemore would be burned to the ground as a reprisal for the Kiloskehan ambush, and 'pilgrims, stall-holders and tramps all made a hasty exit'.[6] Within a few days relative normality had once more returned to Templemore. Commandant Jimmy Leahy later said that, 'The abnormal conditions brought about by Jimmy Walsh and his miracles had lasted for three weeks.'[7]

In January 1922 the widow of Constable Noonan and the mother of Constable Flood appeared in Nenagh Circuit Court during compensation award hearings. Mrs Noonan gave evidence that her first husband had been killed during the Great War, leaving her widowed with two young children. Her marriage to Edward Noonan, a former Grenadier Guardsman who had been wounded during the Great War, had resulted in the birth of a son. Her mother Mrs Stutter, who owned a boarding house in London, told the court that the death of her second husband had left her daughter 'prostrate for about a month, as they had been very happy'. The judge awarded compensation to the amount of £5,000.[8] Mrs Kate Flood gave evidence that the death of her son Terence had caused severe hardship, as most of her 13 children had either died or emigrated. She had been totally reliant on the money Edward had sent home as the family farm did not provide enough income to live on. She was awarded £600 for her loss. At the same hearing Constable Ferris, who survived the Kiloskehan ambush, told the court that he had received a scalp wound when a bullet pierced his cap. Described as one of the 'old stock of the Royal Irish Constabulary' as he had joined the force in 1894, his barrack roommate Constable Walsh gave evidence that Ferris had suffered nightmares following the ambush and often shouted 'assassins' in his sleep. He was awarded £600 compensation.[9]

Commandant Seán Harling of the 2nd Battalion, Dublin Brigade, Fianna Éireann, worked as a courier for Michael Collins and Dáil Éireann from 1919–21. In later life he recalled that in 1920, 'Mick Collins asked me to get the train down to Tipperary and bring this statue back to him'.[10] Complaints had been made directly to Collins by members of the Roman Catholic clergy that IRA Volunteers in the county had manufactured a statue that bled 'to raise money to buy guns for the IRA'. Harling stated that the clergy had 'kicked up murder about it' to Collins, so he was dispatched to Tipperary to bring back one of the statues for examination. It was alleged that the internal mechanism of an alarm clock had been concealed inside a statue. This mechanism was connected to rubber fountain pen inserts containing sheep's blood. When the clock struck a certain time it would send a spurt of blood through the statue's heart, thus giving the impression that the statue was bleeding. When Harling returned to Dublin, Michael Collins examined the statue before he 'took hold of the statue and banged it off the side of the desk, and of course out fell the works on the alarm clock. I knew it, said Collins … so that was the end of the bleeding statue.'[11] This was not the first occasion that religious statues had been used in connection with the Irish revolution. Just before the 1916 Rising, Volunteers in Donegal arranged to have three French machine guns imported from London. The large and cumbersome weapons were to be concealed inside life-sized religious statues specially ordered for this purpose, delivered to a parish priest in Donegal. The plan failed, however, when the French government seized the weapons for use on the Western Front by their own soldiers.[12]

The brief interlude which had seen Templemore become an internationally famous place of pilgrimage ended abruptly with the Kiloskehan ambush, which brought about a violent renewal of hostilities. The situation worsened considerably on 28 October 1920 when a military convoy carrying soldiers of the Northamptonshire Regiment travelling from Templemore was ambushed at Thomastown, near Tipperary town. The gun battle which followed between the IRA and the military lasted for almost an hour. Three soldiers – Privates Crummey and Short of the Northamptonshire Regiment and Lance Corporal Hobbs of the Royal Engineers – were killed. Crummey was originally from Nenagh in Tipperary and had spent his childhood in the town workhouse, but met his death in his native county at the hands of fellow Tipperary men, aged just seventeen. He was subsequently buried with full military honours in St Michael's Catholic cemetery in Tipperary town.

The military claimed that many casualties had been sustained by the IRA during the Thomastown ambush, but only one Volunteer, Michael Fitzpatrick, was wounded.[13] Volunteer James Kilmartin was impressed by the bravery of one soldier who stood in the middle of the road firing at the attackers with two automatic pistols. He seemed to have a 'charmed life' as he was not downed by the rifle fire of the Volunteers, who believed that he may have been wearing body armour.[14] Following the ambush an extensive manhunt took place in the surrounding countryside, which involved the use of bloodhounds.[15] Detailed accounts of the ambush were carried in newspapers in Northamptonshire, which reported that 'much bitterness prevailed amongst the rank and file of the regiment at the loss of their comrades'.[16] This anger manifested itself in reprisal attacks carried out in Templemore and Tipperary town. For the second time in only a few weeks, Templemore was badly damaged in a reprisal attack. Masked men appeared on the streets shouting anti-Sinn Féin slogans, including 'we will have revenge' and 'up the Black and Tans'.[17]

One witness described the scene as 'a hell let loose of pandemonium, panic and uproar – a saturnalia of desperate, though apparently disciplined men'.[18] A dozen armed men forced their way into another shop shouting 'we are the Black and Tans' and demanded to know from the owners where their two adult sons were, but fortunately for them perhaps, the young men were not at home.[19] Over seventy premises had their windows broken and two shops, Kelly's grocery and Smith's bicycle shop, were completely destroyed by fire. An American journalist who was visiting the town reported that, 'Raiders proceeded to array themselves in women's hats, blouses, skirts and lingerie, some masking themselves with aprons.'[20] Musical instruments were taken from another shop, and the strains of these instruments accompanied volleys of rifle fire as soldiers moved through the town wrecking everything in their path.

County Inspector Dunlop informed Dublin Castle that the Thomastown ambush had led to 'reprisals by armed and disguised men, resulting in serious loss of property', but no reference was made to the identity of those who carried out the reprisal.[21] The *Freemans Journal* reported that, 'Strange as it may seem, the police barracks was availed of by many persons as a place of refuge and safety during the outbreak.'[22] Uniformed police, including Black and Tans, forced the drunken soldiers back to barracks and helped to put out the fires. Local shopkeeper Mrs Brennan said that police had helped to put out flames in her shop and acted 'in a very plucky manner, and deserved the highest praise'.[23] The police were subsequently thanked by the local urban district council for their actions.[24] Valuable assistance was also provided by both the Roman Catholic and Protestant clergy based in the town. Hugh Martin of the *Daily News* returned to Templemore after first covering the story of the miracles and apparitions in August. He reported that while 'riotously drunken soldiers were breaking windows and burning buildings, the police including Black and Tans displayed considerable gallantry in fighting the fires … although they seemed unable or unwilling to quell the riot'.[25] The events in Templemore were raised in the House of Commons when Chief Secretary Sir Hamar Greenwood announced an inquiry into the events of 29 October 1920. He stated, however, that newspaper descriptions of the incident as the 'sack-ing of Templemore, were not in accordance with the facts'. He went on to say that the local police had no information as to who the perpetrators of the outrage were.

Vice Commandant Edward McGrath of the IRA recalled in later life the night of the reprisal as the funeral carriage of Terence McSwiney was due to pass through Templemore train station on the way to Cork city. About 1.30 p.m. that afternoon he received information from a sympathetic postman that the military planned to wreck Templemore that night. McGrath believed that it was not a case of drunken and infuriated soldiers running amok, but that they acted on the orders of officers who accompanied them.[26] Reprisals carried out by crown forces provoked local and international criticism and led to the perception as articulated in *The Times* of London that, 'either the executive authority regards them with a certain leniency or that it is powerless to stop them'.[27]

In January 1922 compensation award hearings took place at Nenagh Circuit Court for damage caused during the reprisal attack which took place in Templemore on 29 October 1920. Draper John Kennedy gave evidence that because of the 'supposed miraculous bleeding of statues', Templemore had attracted large crowds of pilgrims from all parts of Ireland, giving the impression that the town would 'become a city, or a second Lourdes'. He had greatly increased his purchases to cater for the number of pilgrims, and was awarded £5,500 for damage to his premises and loss of stock.[28] The deteriorating situation in Munster was attributed by the inspector general to an IRA conspiracy to break down British government in Ireland.[29] The government suppressed Sinn Féin and what were described as 'kindred associations' under the Criminal Law and Procedure (Ireland) Act. In the martial law areas of Clare and Tipperary, public assemblies, including fairs and markets, unless with a permit, were prohibited under the Defence of the Realm regulations.[30] Upon leaving Templemore for the last time, Hugh Martin noted that such tactics and the policy of reprisals 'helped to manufacture physical-force men out of peaceable citizens'.[31]

Several key events took place on the national stage during this period which had profound implications for the conflict in Tipperary. In Dublin, 18-year-old medical student Kevin Barry was executed in Mountjoy Jail for his involvement in an attack on a military patrol which resulted in the death of a soldier. His youthfulness and background made him a cause célèbre and generated widespread sympathy, thus adding to the pressure on government to reach a negotiated settlement. Seán Treacy, who had taken part in the Soloheadbeg ambush and was a key figure in the development of the militant nationalist movement in Tipperary, was shot dead by the Auxiliary Division at Talbot Street in Dublin on 14 October. Three other people, including a child, were also killed in the crossfire. In London the Lord Mayor of Cork, Terence MacSwiney, died on 25 October after spending seventy-three days on hunger strike. Newspapers reported that one of the bleeding statues from Templemore had been brought to MacSwiney in Brixton Prison, and permission had been given to place it in his cell.[32]

On 2 November RIC Constable McCarthy was shot and seriously wounded while on patrol in Nenagh. That night two houses belonging to prominent Sinn Féin members in the town were destroyed in reprisal. Following these incidents Lieutenant Henry James Hambleton, intelligence officer of the 1st Battalion of the Northamptonshire Regiment from Summerhill Barracks in Nenagh, was targeted for assassination. It was alleged that Hambleton had threatened to shoot Nenagh priest Fr O' Halloran, who had denounced the tactics employed by the military and RIC from the pulpit.[33] Commandant Seán Gaynor stated that the IRA decided to kill Hambleton as he had a reputation for being 'an extremely bad pill'.[34] On 4 November Hambleton was seen by members of the Volunteers who were working in fields, travelling by motorcycle from Nenagh towards regimental headquarters at Richmond Barracks in Templemore. An ambush was hastily arranged for Lissatunny, a mile outside Nenagh. As Hambleton returned from Templemore a number of shots were fired, causing him to lose control of his motorcycle and crash. He returned fire despite being badly wounded, but was shot again as he lay on the ground. Volunteer Edward Ryan, a member of the ambush party, reported that his dying words were, 'You bastards, you got me at last.'[35] When his body was searched for documents he was found to be wearing steel body armour, as worn by British troops in the trenches during the latter part of the Great War.

The official history of the Northamptonshire Regiment stated that in his role as intelligence officer, Hambleton had shown himself to be 'absolutely fearless and had become a marked man'.[36] His death was viewed by the local IRA, however, as 'good riddance', and they noted that some RIC men in Nenagh subsequently appeared to suffer from 'cold feet'.[37] Following this killing the cyclical pattern of ambush followed by reprisal continued. When Hambleton's remains arrived at Summerhill Barracks, some of the men under his command set fire to several premises, including a local creamery.[38] Shots were fired, grenades thrown and broken glass littered the streets. The cost of the damage was subsequently estimated at over £2,000. Prominent businessmen united with Protestant and Roman Catholic clergy to send a telegraph to Dublin Castle asking for protection for townspeople, who were described as being 'panic-stricken'.[39]

Referring to the ambush in the House of Commons, Sir Hamer Greenwood said that Hambleton had been 'shot over the heart by a bullet, and his left forearm almost blown off'.[40] Greenwood did admit that troops got out of hand for a short time, 'despite the efforts of the officers, and committed a certain amount of destruction before they were again got in hand'. He went on to say that Hambleton was 'one of the most popular officers in the battalion, his men loved him … they would have shot and killed and have burned the town of Nenagh to the ground, and there are many men who would say they would have been justified in doing so, but I do not'.[41]

John O'Brien and Thomas O'Brien, members of the Nenagh IRA company, were killed during the reprisal attack. Other Volunteers alleged that both men had been bayoneted to death in the back of a military lorry.[42] The military, however, claimed that they had been shot while 'trying to escape'.[43] Hambleton was buried on 10 November at St Martin's Church, Exminster, Devon. His memorial plaque reads, 'To the glory of God & in memory of a very gallant gentleman Henry James Hambleton … assassinated by Irish rebels near Nenagh, 4th November 1920.'[44]

The road from Templemore to Nenagh via the town of Borrisoleigh where Hambleton died was one of the most dangerous in Ireland during the 1919–22 period. Twenty-one miles in length, the road meandered through valleys and wooded countryside, making it a perfect location for sniper attacks, ambushes and the placement of landmines. The Northamptonshire Regiment had a large garrison at Summerhill Barracks in Nenagh, and the county inspector of the RIC was also based in Nenagh. This meant that frequent trips between Templemore and Nenagh were necessary for both the military and police. Many IRA ambushes took place on this road, which soldiers derisively called 'happy valley' or 'the valley of death'.[45] To deter the IRA from carrying out ambushes, the military adopted the tactic of carrying 'prominent Sinn Féiners on all convoys'.[46] The RIC expressed doubts that this practice would have any effect and feared it would be counterproductive, merely causing Volunteers to go on the run. At Christmas 1920 a large IRA party led by Jim Stapleton ambushed a military convoy at Collaun, near Borrisoleigh. The convoy consisted of fifteen lorries and 150 soldiers. This engagement lasted for 5 hours until the IRA withdrew, fearing the arrival of reinforcements from Templemore. Following the ambush, the route was no longer used by the military and police.

The year 1920 had been one of extraordinary events. The few weeks of the Templemore Miracles had provided a brief respite from violence, but despite this more policemen died in the county during 1920 than in any other year of the war of independence. In December 1920 IRA Commandant Edward McGrath was interned in Richmond Barracks under the provisions of the Restoration of Order in Ireland Act. He was visited in his cell by Captain Hubert Phipps, MC, intelligence officer of the 1st Battalion, the officer who had replaced Hambleton. McGrath was told that he would be brought out as a hostage on convoys. He was subsequently taken out on several occasions and forced to walk in front of convoys as they advanced through the countryside between Templemore and Nenagh.[47] During one ambush McGrath suffered the discomfort of having to take cover while his IRA colleagues fired shots at the convoy, unwittingly placing him in grave danger. During the incident McGrath had a close-up view of the soldiers' reaction to this form of guerrilla warfare, and stated in later life that they were 'simply terrified'.[48]

Shortly after the Kiloskehan ambush had taken place it was reported that Jimmy Walsh had left Templemore and was staying in Pallaskenry, County Limerick, with the 'Salesian community at their newly opened house in Copeswood'.[49] This situation had arisen when Fr Aloysius Sutherland brought an ill priest called Fr Leaver and a deaf lay-aspirant to the order called Carroll to Templemore to meet Walsh in the hope that they could be cured. Walsh told them to do a seven-day novena and donate money to the church. Fr Sutherland was not at all impressed, but nonetheless agreed to a request from Fr Kiely, parish priest of Templemore, to take Walsh to Copeswood as he had been creating 'quite a stir with his holiness and gift of cures'.[50] Some days later a Salesian called Grey collected Walsh from Limerick train station and took him to Pallaskenry. This may have been Fr Edward Grey (1890–1978), who came from Templemore and was one of the Grey family of George's Street, where statues had also been reported to have moved and bled in the presence of Jimmy Walsh.[51]

When it became known that the 'holy boy' Jimmy Walsh was in Copeswood, 'the lame, the blind and the deaf of the locality came to him to be cured'. On one occasion, when Fr Sutherland returned from Limerick he found that statues in the school which Walsh had access to had blood on them, but a statue that he had kept locked in his own bedroom did not. Sutherland became suspicious and Walsh was 'hustled away before there would be a riot'.[52] By November 1920 newspapers began to report that public interest in Templemore had died down and previously reported cures were now being discredited.[53] People who had been named in newspapers as having been cured 'were astonished to see their names among the cures'. While some said that they had experienced improvement, in no case investigated by newspapers was there evidence of a positive cure. One person who had discarded their crutches had begun to use them again, and another stated to have been cured was now unable to leave their bed. Other reported cures were found to have been absolutely groundless.[54] Reference was also made to the fact that senior clergy, including Monsignor Innocent Ryan of Cashel and the parish priest of Templemore, Fr Kiely, had warned people against a 'too hasty belief'. The fact that so many reporters and correspondents were in Ireland covering the conflict was cited as a reason why the story of the Templemore Miracles gained such worldwide publicity; there was enormous demand for 'Irish copy … everything that happens and some things that do not happen are copiously written up'.[55] The noted Australian humanitarians and writers Joice M. Nankivell and her husband Sydney Loch visited Ireland while they were writing a book on the conflict. Referring to the situation in Templemore, they wrote:

> The miraculous bleeding which caused Ireland momentarily to hold her breath, as if supernatural intervention were coming, became a nine days' wonder, and then was no more. This week it was, next week it was not. Perhaps it was the arrival of the *Daily Sketch* reporter with his gimlet eye and his camera.[56]

In December 1920 Thomas Dwan wrote to the *Nenagh Guardian* newspaper claiming that a crucifix in his house which had bled in August had 'sweated to a great degree, and that the manifestation was witnessed by several residents'.[57] The statues were still on display in the window of Dwan's house, and requests for water from the well at Curraheen had been received from all over the world, including Bombay in India. That was the last reference made to the bleeding statues or Templemore Miracles in local or national newspapers. Rumours spread in Tipperary that a man called 'Stack from Pudding Lane [now Kincora Avenue] in Thurles had applied red paint to some statues overnight'. The

1911 census does show that a man called Gerald J. Stack, described as a 'religious teacher', lived at 161 Pudding Lane with five other men, also described as religious teachers. The head of the household was listed as 'Richard Wall, Superior'.[58]

On 28 June 1921, the last large-scale operation by the IRA against crown forces in north Tipperary took place when the heavily fortified RIC barracks in Borrisoleigh village was attacked. The barracks was of strategic importance as it was located on the road between Nenagh and Thurles. The barracks had been fortified with the installation of steel shutters on all doors and windows, and sandbags, booby traps and barbed wire surrounded the perimeter. Thirty-three former army officers who had served in the Royal Engineers and other specialised regiments had been recruited to the RIC, and given the role and title of 'defence of barrack sergeants'. They were not used for regular policing duties but worked exclusively on such defensive measures.

While these provided a measure of safety to individual policemen, it made their quarters claustrophobic and cramped. To venture outside risked death, but to remain inside brought the threat of siege or other forms of attack. Constabulary reports for the summer of 1920 highlight significant levels of demoralisation because of the boycott, with some policemen even openly calling for the RIC to be disbanded. The inspector general reported that conditions were irksome, depressing and hazardous, a strain which few bodies of men, however highly disciplined, could be expected to bear.[59]

As with previous attacks on terraced barracks such as those at Kilcommon and Rearcross, the usual IRA tactics were employed during the Borrisoleigh attack. The intention was to gain access to the barracks roof via the premises next door, remove some roof slates, pour petrol through the hole and set the barracks on fire, thus forcing the police to abandon it. In Borrisoleigh, however, the RIC had received information about the impending attack and had booby-trapped the upstairs section of Maher's public house next door. The IRA had their own intelligence and knew that a trap had been set by the police, so switched tactics. Local IRA commander Jim Stapleton decided to use a rudimentary 'allowee' bomb commonly used by the IRA. These were manufactured by taking a stick of gelignite and wrapping it in a coating of sticky mud. A fuse was lit and if thrown with accuracy, the bomb would stick to the building before detonating. In the days leading up to the attack, over thirty local Volunteers were assigned to the manufacture of such bombs and up to 400 IRA men from all three Tipperary brigades took part in the attack itself.[60]

On the evening of the attack all roads leading into Borrisoleigh were barricaded; trenches were dug and telephone wires cut. Parties of Volunteers lay in wait at disparate locations, as it was expected that reinforcements would be summoned by the Borrisoleigh garrison when the attack commenced. Diversionary sniper attacks were also planned for police stations at Gurtaderrybeg, Templetouhy and Barnane. The main attack began at 11.00 p.m. when rifle fire was directed at the barracks and the bombs thrown. The barracks soon caught fire but the flames quickly died out. More bombs were thrown with similar results, and Stapleton realised that the barracks was not going to be easily set ablaze. The police inside the barracks sent up Verey flares to summon assistance from Templemore, but none was forthcoming as it was feared that such reinforcements would be lured into an ambush. As dawn approached, IRA commanders decided to end the attack by a pre-arranged signal, the ringing of the bell in the Roman Catholic church. The signal had been deliberately chosen by Jim Stapleton to cause maximum annoyance to the local parish priest, a vocal opponent of the IRA.[61]

In the period leading up to the attack, farm labourer and former soldier Patrick Meagher had been executed by the IRA as he had been seen socialising with policemen and ignored warnings to cease doing so. His body was found by early morning mass-goers, with the usual notice of 'executed by the IRA, spies and informers beware' attached.[62] This followed the deaths in February 1921 of two men from Templemore, James Maher and Patrick O'Meara, who had been abducted and executed. Their bodies were left on the road with similarly worded signs attached.[63] It was reported by the RIC that they had been executed on suspicion of being friendly with, and giving information to, the police as they were former British soldiers. The county inspector stated this to be untrue, adding that, 'these two men never gave any information … and were absolutely useless to us'.[64] As Jimmy Walsh had been viewed as a possible spy following his interrogation by Dan Breen, he was fortunate to escape a similar fate.

On 30 June 1921, 21-year-old Constable Joseph Bourke was shot dead while standing at the door of Templemore RIC barracks. A former soldier from Cork who had joined the police in 1920, the exact circumstances of his death were shrouded in mystery, and no details were released by official sources.[65] One newspaper subsequently reported that RIC Constable William Sheehan had been arrested and was in custody at the military barracks in Templemore in connection with the death of Bourke.[66] In August 1921 a court-martial took place at Victoria Barracks in Cork and Sheehan was charged with the 'wilful murder' of Burke. Medical evidence was given that Sheehan had a 'delusion of persecution' and he had told doctors that he was being 'tormented by everybody'.[67] The court-martial accepted that Sheehan was unable to stand trial due to insanity, and he was remanded in custody to be dealt with according to military regulations.[68] He was subsequently committed to Broadmoor Asylum in England.[69] Such cases illustrate the strain that the RIC was under at this stage of the conflict. The inspector general noted the sharp decline in living conditions, the ever-present danger and being subjected to the appeals of parents and their families to leave the force; 'they could do little more than defend themselves and their barracks. Their lives were a misery.'[70]

When the Anglo-Irish truce began at 12 noon on Monday 11 July 1921, it initially brought a degree of peace to a country ravaged by conflict. It was an uneasy peace, however, and both sides stood in readiness to recommence hostilities if the truce collapsed. The IRA was now referred to for the first time as the 'Irish army' in British government correspondence, giving the militant movement the status and recognition it sought. Deputy Inspector General Walsh of the Royal Irish Constabulary warned his men that extremists 'may commit serious breaches of the truce … but responsible Sinn Féin leaders now have a direct and immediate common interest with the British government in maintaining law and order'.[71] In Tipperary, the county inspector reported on apparent breaches of the ceasefire which saw 'well-known murderers of police parading at will in front of the comrades of those who have been murdered'.[72] Officers of the IRA began to appear openly in public wearing military uniform, and the movement took full advantage of the opportunity to recruit, drill and train. At 2.30 a.m. on 6 December 1921, after a prolonged period of negotiation, a treaty was signed by representatives of the British government led by Prime Minister Lloyd George and Colonial Secretary Winston Churchill.

The Irish provisional government delegation included Michael Collins, Arthur Griffith and Cathal Brugha.

Gormanstown in County Meath was chosen as the depot where all members of the RIC would gather to formally be dispersed. The Auxiliary Division was the first to be disbanded, and the last of its 1,243 members left Ireland on 25 January 1922. Black and Tans, who were members of the regular RIC but had been recruited in England since 1919, were the next group to be dealt with, followed by policemen who had already been serving in the force prior to 1919. In Tipperary, the entire county force was ordered to proceed to Gormanstown in March 1922. The Constabulary (Ireland) Act of 1922 came before parliament on 8 April and set a date of 31 August 1922 for the complete disbandment of the RIC. It also enshrined in legislation the provisions made in terms of pensions and gratuities. Pending the passing of this legislation, a formal disbandment parade took place on 4 April 1922 at the Phoenix Park Depot, the spiritual home of the RIC, which had been built as a training depot for the constabulary in 1842. At the conclusion of this parade, the Royal Irish Constabulary effectively ceased to exist.

Editorialising about the disbandment of the force, the *Irish Times* stated that a force which had given 'magnificent service to the Empire was not only being disbanded, but is being sent virtually into exile'.[73] Describing the passing of the RIC into history, Sir Hamar Greenwood stated in the House of Commons that disbandment had been inevitable in consequence of the treaty, stating that, 'as an imperial force they were born, and as an imperial force they wished to die'.[74] The departure from the country of the British garrison in Ireland also had significant economic consequences for many villages, towns and cities. On 9 December 1921, the *Irish Times* predicted that the withdrawal of the military from the garrison towns of Ireland would be a source of profound regret and that 'towns which owed the greater part of their trade to the military … would now be hard hit unless some compensating factor is supplied'.[75] Hundreds of police barracks, courthouses and other symbols of British governance had been destroyed, and those that remained standing had been evacuated. In common with other garrison towns, the populace of Templemore had maintained a close social and economic relationship with the occupants of Richmond Barracks for over 100 years, and there were serious economic and social consequences when the army departed.

Describing the handover of Richmond to IRA Volunteers on behalf of the Irish provisional government, the official history of the Northamptonshire Regiment caustically described them as a 'motley force calling itself the Irish army'.[76] When marching from barracks to the train station, however, it was noted by soldiers that, 'The enthusiasm of the civil population, after their previous attitude towards British troops, was extraordinary.'[77] As part of the final process of withdrawal from Ireland, the entire contents of Richmond Barracks were sold by public auction.[78] On 25 February 1922, the *Nenagh Guardian* reported that the withdrawal of British troops from the Curragh camp had led to serious unemployment in the town of Kildare and surrounding area, with over 400 men losing their jobs in one week following the final departure of soldiers from local garrisons.[79]

After Jimmy Walsh had left Templemore and Ireland never to return, members of his family continued to deal with the consequences of what had taken place during August and September 1920. Jimmy's sister Sarah worked as a household servant in the Thurles area and was known as 'the saint's sister', with a reputation for being devoutly religious herself. She was unable, for example, to pass a painting of the sacred heart in the kitchen of her workplace in the Lyons family home at Turtulla without bowing and kneeling to pray. On one occasion while serving lunch to workmen, she complained that they were 'no good for anything except drawing water'. One of the workmen called Willie Fahy replied flippantly, 'Maybe so Sarah, but we never sold or blessed any of it!'[80] In the immediate aftermath of the miracles, a local insurance agent called Worthington was passing by Mary Walsh's garden and witnessed local people ask her if this were the 'home of the Saint's mother'? She replied, 'tis, and ye may kiss my arse'! Mr Worthington enjoyed regaling people with this story, but was regarded by local people as a natural sceptic of Roman Catholic superstitions, given that he was a member of the Church of Ireland.[81]

Australia: 'Alone in the World!'[1]

On 31 March 1922, the steamship *Ormuz*, a vessel of the Orient line, sailed from the Port of London to Melbourne in the state of Victoria, Australia. Passengers included 18-year-old Jimmy Walsh, who listed his profession, occupation or calling on the passenger manifest as 'student'. Also on board the *Ormuz* were his brother Patrick, aged 27, a 'farmer', and his sister Bridget, 19, who was listed as a 'domestic servant'.[2] When he arrived in Australia Jimmy, who had been named James Kevin Walsh at birth, began to use variations of his name including Kevin Walshe with an 'e', J.K. Walshe or Kevin Benedict Walshe. This allowed him a certain degree of anonymity while at the same time not actually using a false identity. Nothing is known of the activities of Walsh until February 1925, when Catholic priest Reverend T.J. Little of Fern Tree Gully parish in the city of Melbourne wrote to the Benedictine monastery at New Norcia in Western Australia on behalf of a parishioner who was seeking information about how to join the Benedictine order. That parishioner was Jimmy Walsh.

New Norcia, Australia's only monastic town, is located 129km from Perth and over 3,400km from Melbourne, where Walsh lived. In 1844 two Benedictine monks, Dom Léandre Fonteinne from France and Irishman John Gorman, were assigned as missionaries to the newly appointed first Roman Catholic Bishop of Perth, the Right Reverend John Brady, who originally came from County Cavan in Ireland. Brady arrived in Sydney in 1838 with the first large group of Irish clergy to reach Australia. His parishioners initially consisted primarily of Irish convicts consigned to work for local landowners. Believing that the indigenous Aboriginal population could be evangelised, Brady travelled to Rome in 1843 to petition for more priests and missionaries to be sent to Australia. The monastery at New Norcia was subsequently established in 1847 with this intent.[3] In his letter Father Little stated that Walsh was 'a recent convert in whom I am interested … he was received into the Roman Catholic Church several weeks ago. He seems to have a bent towards the Benedictine order and as far as I can judge, has a calling to the ecclesiastical life.'[4]

Little went on to say that the young man in question was called 'Kevin Walshe', and both of his parents had been officers in the Salvation Army in England, but were now deceased. Describing him as a Londoner who had been in Australia for three years, he gave his opinion that 'Walshe' was intelligent and had received a 'fair education at primary standard'. Walsh told Father Little the reason he had converted to Roman Catholicism was that while volunteering with the Salvation Army he had helped a fellow member, a lapsed Catholic, regain his faith by arranging for a Catholic priest to hear his confession before he died.[5] The Salvation Army was founded in 1865 in London by minister William Booth, who founded a church, the East London Christian Mission, specifically for the poor, the homeless, the hungry and the destitute. The archives of the Salvation Army International Heritage Centre in London have no records which show that Jimmy Walsh was a member of, or volunteered with, the Salvation Army either in the UK or Australia.[6]

In reality, Jimmy Walsh's parents were farm labourers from the village of Drom near Templemore, County Tipperary. Walsh had been baptised into the Roman Catholic faith at Inch parish church near Templemore on 17 February 1904 by Archbishop John Mary Harty of the Diocese of Cashel and Emly. Harty also confirmed him at Drom parish church in February 1915, and it was to Dr Harty that Walsh had confessed his part in feigning the Templemore Miracles in 1920.

Continuing his letter to New Norcia, Father Little commented that Walsh had 'read himself into the faith … his dispositions are most spiritual, his talks and letters would cause me to think he had known the Roman Catholic religion all his life'. Little was unaware that Jimmy Walsh had been born and raised as a devout Catholic, so had in fact known the religion for all of his life. Speaking of the 'burning desire' of Walsh to become a priest and preach the word of God, Father Little went on to say that he was currently 'looking after boys in a Methodist training home, a good deal of which he had done when in the army'. There are no records which show that Jimmy Walsh ever served in either the British or Australian armies. The archives of the Uniting Church in Western Australia have no evidence that Walsh was employed by the Methodist Church in Australia in any capacity. The Uniting Church in Australia (UCA) was established in 1977, when most congregations of the Methodist Church of Australasia, the Presbyterian Church of Australia and the Congregational Union of Australia came together under the Basis of Union.[7] Concluding his letter to New Norcia, Father Little signed off by saying that, 'Mr Walsh has no relatives in Australia, he is alone in the world!' In reality, when he had travelled to Australia in 1922, he had been accompanied by his siblings Patrick and Bridget.

On 8 April 1925, Father Little wrote again to the abbott of New Norcia, stating that he had not received a response to his previous letter and 'Mr Walsh was most anxious to get news'. Father Little had 'no hesitation in recommending him as a fit subject for your community'. He also said that Walsh was at present staying with him at the presbytery in Fern Tree Gully, and offered to provide financial assistance if needed to help him achieve his 'laudable final ambition to be a priest of your order'.[8] On 13 April Father Little received a letter from Dom Gerardo Castanares of New Norcia which said that the issue would be considered by the head of the order, Dom Anselm Catalan, 'upon his return from an overseas trip'.[9] In response, Father Little wrote that this news was 'very useful to my young friend', and though it did not 'realise his most ardent aspirations; it has been a source of joy and the harbinger he hopes of a favourable reply on the return of the Lord Abbott from abroad'.[10]

On 25 July the Benedictines received another letter enquiring about the possibility of Jimmy Walsh being admitted to the order. On this occasion, however, the letter did not come from Father Little, but from Brother William, director of the Marist Brother's College in Kilmore, some 74km from the centre of Melbourne. Brother William wrote that 'Kevin Walshe' (*sic*) was a resident boarder of the college, having previously lived in Fern Tree Gully. Brother William enquired what the prospects of his admission were, and queried if the letter which Walsh had received stating that the matter awaited the return of the Dom Catalan was a 'gracious way of putting him off'? Brother William acknowledged that Father Little had already given a full history of the boy, whom he described as an 'ex-Salvationist', and said that while Walsh had received encouragement from another order of priests, his wish was to be a Benedictine. If the order believed that he should try elsewhere, however, 'kindly let me know'. He also described Walsh as a 'good student who has made commendable progress … his ability is an average one'.[11]

In August 1925 Father Little wrote to another member of the Benedictines, Father Gerardo Castanares. He stated that, 'Mr Walshe is as strong, if not stronger, in his determination to become a humble son of Saint Benedict', and was making excellent progress with Latin and other subjects at the Marist College. He concluded, 'I feel that he has a calling to the religious life, an opinion that will be endorsed by others than myself.' He said that the purpose of his letters was to 'know what the prospects for Mr Walsh's admission to New Norcia at the end of the year are so that he may be able to act accordingly relative to the extension of his studies at Kilmore next year or otherwise'.[12]

On New Year's Day 1926, Father Little wrote directly to Abbott Dom Catalan.[13] He referred to Walsh as 'a protégé of mine who is desirous of becoming a priest in your esteemed and illustrious order. He is English by birth, approaching his twenty-second year and is a convert of some twelve months standing.'

Little went on to say that in all of his experience as a priest, he had never come across a convert with such deep religious fervour or insight into the religious life. He went on to say that while Walsh had received many rebuffs since becoming a Roman Catholic it had not discourage him, but revealed a deep religious trait. He wrote that Walsh's 'desire to become a Benedictine is not a mere whim or impulse of religious fervour consequent on his reception into the church, while he is aware of the arduous life he contemplates, he has adopted an unswerving attitude in his desire to become a Benedictine'.

Little finished his letter by again saying that Walsh was 'alone in the world, his parents are dead, he knows of no available relatives'. In reality, his parents Daniel and Mary Walsh were alive and living in Tipperary, and Jimmy had ten siblings, at least two of whom were actually living in Australia at that time. Father Little also gave the names of several referees who would be glad to write letters supporting the application to join the Benedictines. These included Brother William from the Marist College in Kilmore, Father Patrick Gleeson, parish priest of Kilmore, and Father Joseph King, parish priest of Our Lady's in East Brunswick, Melbourne.

Little received a response from Dom Catalan saying that consideration could not be given to admitting Jimmy Walsh to New Norcia at that time as the monastery was operating at full capacity. Father Little replied that while both he and Walsh were 'naturally disappointed at the nature of your reply … I gather that the impossible present did not make for an impossible future'.[14] Father Little concluded his letter by stating:

> My young friend still hopes that he will yet achieve his lofty aspiration and is buoyed under the hope that in reaching the educational standards required, and a vacancy arising at New Norcia, his ardent desire to become a humble follower of St Benedict may be realised. Would you give him hope for encouragement in his holy aspiration?

On 12 February 1926, Jimmy Walsh wrote directly to Dom Catalan for the first time.[15] Using headed paper from the Marist College in Kilmore, he used the name Kevin Benedict Walshe for the first time. He had been using the surname Walshe with an 'e' since he had arrived in Australia four years earlier. A copy of a baptismal certificate in the author's possession which was sent from his home parish in Tipperary to Jimmy Walsh in Australia clearly shows that the letter 'e' was manually added to the name Walsh where it appeared in three places on that certificate. This was in reference not only to Jimmy himself, but also to his father Daniel and sister Johanna where their names appeared as witnesses on the certificate.[16]

In his letter, Walsh apologised to Dom Catalan for 'taking the liberty of addressing you directly, but my confessor advised me to write to you'. He referred to the numerous letters written on his behalf by Father Little and also of his 'desire to become a Benedictine which seems to grow each day'. Referring to the fact that New Norcia was at present full, he wrote, 'May God's will be done. When I pray God to enlighten me, to choose another order, I seem to hear an interior voice ever singing "thou must be a Benedictine". And I believe that in spite of my unworthiness, that God will have pity on me.'

Pleading to be given consideration when his present studies were completed, he finished his letter by saying that he 'would persevere with God's help and the assistance of your prayers ... I would be pleased to know if there is any reasonable chance of my been [*sic*] accepted when I finish my studies?'

There was no further correspondence for over nine months until Walsh wrote again to Dom Catalan in October 1926.[17] This letter was addressed from the presbytery of St Mary's parish church at Dandenong, also in the state of Victoria. In September 1926 Father Little had been appointed as parish priest of Dandenong, 17km from his previous parish of Fern Tree Gully. Walsh stated that he had been 'living with my confessor' Father Little since his reception into the Roman Catholic Church, and that he 'approves of my desires and thinks that I have a vocation'. Significantly, Walsh stated that during the previous week, 'I have had an audience with his grace Dr Mannix, he advised me to try again and enquire if there is any possibility of my being received?' Dr Mannix, the Archbishop of Melbourne, is a very significant figure both in Australian and Irish history, and his involvement shows that Walsh had obtained support from influential figures within the Roman Catholic hierarchy in his efforts to obtain entry to New Norcia as a postulant.[18] Walsh ended his letter with the words, 'I am, my dear Lord, your obedient servant in Jesus Christ, Kevin Benedict Walshe.'

Having been asked to supply further information about his educational achievements, Walsh wrote again to Dom Catalan in November that year, stating that he had received a good primary education. He listed the following subjects he was studying, 'with the object in view of becoming a Benedictine priest': Latin, French, English, history, geography, arithmetic, physics, chemistry, algebra, geography, Greek and Roman history.[19] He also wrote that a 'kind friend has offered to pay for my education', perhaps referring to Father Little, who had stated in a previous letter to New Norcia that he would be willing to provide financial assistance to Jimmy Walsh should it be beneficial to his application for admission. Walsh referred again to Dr Mannix, 'from whom I get weekly confession … and who thought if I made a retreat at your monastery it would benefit me a great deal'. He signed off, 'Begging a remembrance in your holy mass, I am my dear Lord Abbott, your obedient servant in Jesus Christ, Kevin Benedict Walshe.'

In January 1927 Walsh wrote again to Dom Catalan, saying that Father Little, 'my spiritual director, has asked me to address you, in order that he may arrange for me to continue my studies'.[20] It was now almost two years since Father Little had first enquired about the possibility of Jimmy Walsh joining the Benedictines, and Walsh requested forgiveness for the numerous letters written both by Father Little and himself, saying:

> Forgive me my dear Lord, if I seem too anxious about my future, but I am sure you will understand that my intentions are good and arise from a burning desire to give myself to God. I feel sure that Jesus is calling me to the religious life and I am prepared to go where he wants me.

Walsh received a response from New Norcia suggesting that it would improve his chances of admission if he were to receive additional tuition in certain subjects, including Latin. Spanish was also strongly recommended as it was widely spoken in New Norcia, with many of the monks being from Spain. In his reply, Walsh thanked Dom Catalan for his 'encouraging letter, and I have arranged to take up the study of Spanish next week'. He went on to say that as Spanish was not currently taught in secondary schools or colleges, that Father Little:

has arranged with the Spanish consul, or rather with the consul of the Argentine Republic who has been a professor in one of our universities, of your language, and he has kindly consented to teach me. Regarding Latin, I have a fairly good knowledge of it, and I will complete my matriculation examination early in June.[21]

In June 1927 Dom Catalan received a letter from the principal of St Kevin's College in Melbourne, Brother Claver Marlow, stating that:

Mr Kevin B. Walshe has made considerable progress in his Latin studies and recently passed an examination that approximates to the Leaving Certificate or Matriculation standard. The authors studied were Titus Livius book IX, the History of Rome, Book 9, and Horace, Odes III.

This letter shows that Walsh was now receiving tuition at the Christian Brothers school at Toorak in Melbourne. In August 1927 Jimmy Walsh sent his final letter to Dom Catalan pleading to be admitted to New Norcia:[22]

I implore and beg of you for the love of Jesus and Mary to grant my long-felt prayer and to allow me to come to you quickly. In this I am urged by the desire that has been constantly with me day and night since my reception into the church, to do what I believe is God's holy will. Instinctively I feel that I must go to New Norcia or nowhere, as I believe it is God who has kept alive in me this desire in the past, so I look to him and pray to him for my future perseverance.

He finished the letter by saying that, 'I do not know what else I can say to your Lordship in order to plead my cause, I can only implore of you to let me come to you at New Norcia.'

The situation changed dramatically, however, on 5 December 1927 when Dom Catalan received an urgent communication from Father Little who warned him 'on no account whatsoever to admit Walshe as a novice'.[23] Father Little went on to say that he had been:

> deceived by him as also many others. Three weeks ago as a result of an exposure he was found to have had an extraordinary career whereby he had been in some religious houses in Ireland and England and in short was not a convert, had always been a Catholic, and was born in Ireland and not England as alleged. Whilst regretting all that has happened previously, I am glad that his duplicity was discovered before he got to New Norcia.

The 'exposure' referred to by Father Little is not specified in his letter. This would be the last occasion that the Benedictine order would hear of Kevin Benedict Walshe, at least for the time being!

Following this revelation, Jimmy Walsh relocated to Sydney in New South Wales, 900km from his previous home in Melbourne. On 14 June 1929, using the name Kevin Benedict Walshe and the inaccurate date of birth of 17 November 1905 (rather than the actual 16 February 1904), Jimmy Walsh enrolled as a student at Moore Theological College in Newtown, Sydney. He was now studying in preparation for ordination as a minister in the Anglican Church. On his application he stated that he was living at Victoria Street, Sydney, and employed as a teacher. On the question 'have you been engaged in any religious work?', Walsh answered that he had been 'teaching the Aborigines, Western Australia'.[24] The Australian Department of Lands, Planning and Heritage have no records which show that Jimmy Walsh ever had any involvement with teaching the Aboriginal people of Western Australia.

As part of the application process, Walsh provided letters from two referees including the rector of St Stephen's Anglican Church in Newtown, Sydney, the Reverend John Bidwell. He wrote that he had known Walsh for the previous two years and had 'the pleasure of receiving him openly in the church at the morning service when he renounced resolutely the doctrines of the Church of Rome'. As Walsh had done in Victoria State four years earlier, he claimed to have renounced the faith he was baptised into and obtained the support of local clergy and other influential people to support his application for admission to holy orders. Bidwell went on to say that Walsh was a frequent visitor to the rectory, thus giving him ample opportunity to study his character and suitability for ordination. Bidwell concluded that Walsh 'bears an excellent character, is an earnest Christian man, a faithful student of the scriptures and has accepted the truth by conviction'. Concluding his reference, the rector of St Stephen's wrote of his belief that if Walsh were accepted as a candidate for ordination, he would prove to be a 'valuable man and a zealous minister of the gospel'.[25]

Another of Walsh's referees was Alexander James Kilgour, headmaster of Strathfield Grammar and Preparatory School for boys. During a long career as an educationalist, Kilgour acquired a reputation for being a rigid disciplinarian who, unusually for the time, did not use corporal punishment. His teaching was 'excellent, though his standards were inflexible … he had no tolerance for slackers and dullards'.[26] Kilgour wrote that he was personally acquainted with Walsh as he had been 'a member of my staff at Strathfield School for two terms from 1928'.[27] Answering the question 'Does the candidate possess those moral and intellectual qualities required of a candidate for holy orders?', Kilgour stated that, 'to the best of my knowledge, he does'. Kilgour concluded that Walsh was 'industrious, takes an interest in his work, and is neat and tidy in his person'.[28]

Moore College Archives show that Walsh was absent on leave for most of 1931 due to illness. He passed the

Sydney Matriculation examination in 1933, but he did not graduate from Moore, and there is no evidence that he finished his studies or was ordained as an Anglican priest.[29] Regarding his teaching qualifications, there are no records in the state archives of Western Australia, Victoria or New South Wales which show that he received formal qualifications to teach. At that time in Australia, however, teachers in non-government independent or private schools did not require formal qualifications. Notices regarding appointments and transfers in government schools did appear in the main newspapers, but the name of Kevin Walshe or any of the variations he used of that name do not feature in any of these notices.

On 21 September 1932, at Saint Patrick's Roman Catholic Church in Hillside, Sydney, Jimmy Walsh married Doris Ada Hill. Father Aloysius Jeffcott officiated. Aged 21, Doris was seven years younger than Jimmy and had been born in West Tottenham, Middlesex, England, on 15 August 1911. Her father, William George Hill, was a master boot repairer and her mother was Ada Harriett Hill (née Hughes).[30] The Hill family lived at Lane Cove Road, North Sydney, and Doris gave her profession on the marriage certificate as a 'nurse'. Jimmy had met Doris through her sister, Gladys, and their shared interest in the game of tennis. The marriage was witnessed by Gladys Wade (née Hill) and Ada Harriet Hill, mother of the bride.

Fourteen days before she married Jimmy, Doris was baptised into the Roman Catholic faith in the same church, and that ceremony was also performed by Father Jeffcott.[31] Jimmy Walsh lived at The Avenue, Strathfield, Sydney, and listed his occupation as a 'medical undergraduate' on the marriage certificate. He also stated that his father, Daniel Walsh, was a solicitor, whereas both the 1901 and 1911 censuses of Ireland listed his occupation as 'farm labourer'. Jimmy Walsh signed the register using the name James Kevin Walshe. In later life he told his children and grandchildren that he preferred to use his middle name of Kevin rather than his given Christian name of James. He also told them that the reason why he had added an 'e' to his birth surname was because there were so many people called Walsh already listed in the Sydney telephone directory, and he wanted to make his name look different to everyone else's. When talking about why he had left Ireland and emigrated to Australia in 1922, his family were told that he had been a teacher in Ireland during the War of Independence, but when he punished the child of a wealthy local landowner, he was forced to leave the country. In reality Jimmy Walsh was 18 when he emigrated and had been employed as a farm labourer at the time of the Templemore Miracles in 1920, aged only 16.

Despite the fact that he had eleven siblings, the only family member he ever mentioned to his children and grandchildren was his brother Patrick, who had emigrated with him in 1922. Family members recall the importance that Jimmy Walsh placed on religion. Education was also given prominence within the family. He would often quiz his children on their school work and scold them if they did not have satisfactory knowledge of the subject concerned. The marriage of Jimmy Walsh and Doris Hill produced four children: Isobel Margaret (born in December 1933), Elizabeth Mary (May 1937), Graydon Kevin (November 1939) and Graydon Bruce (January 1941). Graydon Kevin died at birth, and his death was the subject of a memorial notice placed by his 'sorrowing parents' which appeared in newspapers on 8 November 1940, the date of his first anniversary.[32]

The circumstances of Graydon's death resulted in a civil court case which attracted much press attention when Doctor George Stanley Thompson, of Macquarie Street, Sydney, sued Jimmy Walsh for unpaid professional fees due for attending at the birth of Graydon. Thompson was involved in several court cases, including one in 1929 when he sued the *Australian Women's Mirror* magazine for libel. An article was published criticising his use of the 'twilight sleep' delivery method in obstetrics. This had first become popular in Germany in the 1880s and was known as '*Dämmerschlaf*', and involved the use of a combination of morphine and scopolamine to relieve the pain of childbirth. Doctor Thompson stated that he was known as the 'twilight sleep man' and his King's

Counsel stated that Thompson had successfully administered this treatment to over 1,000 women. The
magazine claimed, however, that the method has been
'abandoned by medical men and was only used by
quacks'.[33] A number of witnesses were called, including
other doctors and former patients. The jury awarded
Thompson damages to the amount of £250, although
he had sued for £5,000.[34]

By the late 1930s, when Doris gave birth to
Graydon, the method had largely fallen out of use
as many women had suffered severe side effects, and
the rate of foetal death with this method was significantly higher than with normal deliveries, but
Doctor Thompson continued to use the procedure.
During his civil action against Walsh, Thompson gave
evidence that they had agreed a professional fee of
20 guineas, and while 5 guineas had been paid in
advance, Walsh had refused to pay the balance following the death of Graydon. Thompson gave evidence
that during the labour and birth Walsh had been a
'perfect nuisance … wild and crying like a lunatic'.
He also claimed that Walsh and his wife had made
'false statements' about what had taken place during
the period of labour and delivery, and Walsh had
called him a 'proper butcher'. Walsh agreed that he
had used that term and had also called Thompson an
'incompetent quack' when he collected his wife from
the private hospital owned by Thompson, saying that
he would not 'pay him a penny'.

Doris gave evidence that she lost consciousness during labour as chloroform had been administered, and when she awoke she was told that her baby had died. She claimed that she asked Thompson if he had used instruments including the forceps during the birth, to which he replied, 'They are a menace … but if I had used them the results might have been different.' Thompson denied making such remarks. Thompson won his case in the small debts court. Judge Mahoney commented that on the basis of the evidence before him, Thompson could not be found guilty of medical negligence. He was a qualified medical practitioner and no witnesses had been called by Jimmy or Doris Walsh to give evidence on the medical issues which arose during the case. The judge found that the Walshes had failed to pay a debt, and he ordered Jimmy Walsh to pay £18 7s 6d, or 15 guineas, and costs at the rate of £1 per month to Doctor Thompson.[35]

On 24 June 1944, Jimmy Walsh applied to the Australian Register of Copyrights to register a translation of the book *Le Roi des Montagnes* (*King of the Mountains*) as his copyright. A printed copy of the book was supplied with the application, but the name of the author, French novelist Edmond François Valentin About, did not appear, and no reference was made as to his identity. The title given to the Register of Copyrights was '*Le Roi Des Montagnes*, The King of the Mountains, translated by Kevin Walshe, B.A'. The book had first been published in 1857, and the first reference to it having been translated into English appeared in *The Times Literary Supplement* in 1897. What was described as a 'capital translation of the book has been made by Mr Richard Davey, with an introduction by Mr Andrew Lang'.[36]

On 16 August 1944, Walsh's application was returned with a request that it be amended to read 'I am the author of the said literary work'.[37] The application process was designed for the registration of copyright on 'unpublished original literary, dramatic, musical or artistic work'. Jimmy Walsh duly returned the form with the declaration that he was 'the author of the said literary work', signing it 'K. Walshe'. He also initialled the document in several places where he had been requested to do so.[38] The copyright was subsequently registered in his name on 16 January 1945. In his copyright application, Walsh described himself as a 'schoolmaster' and a British subject, and page fifty-two of the printed book which he supplied contained a full page advertisement for 'The Examination Coach', who provided 'expert personal coaching to adults, boys and girls studying for Intermediate, Leaving and Matriculation examinations'. While the advertisement contained no name or other details for the Examination Coach, the address of Leura Road, Double Bay, Sydney, and telephone number of FM4597 was that of Jimmy Walsh. The advert said that the Examination Coach specialised in 'English, French, Latin, German, Greek,

History and Mathematics ... homes visited if desired, terms moderate'.[39]

In the early 1950s, Jimmy Walsh, still using the name Kevin Walshe, was employed as a lay teacher at St Thomas's Christian Brothers school in Lewisham, Sydney. In September 1953 the school was visited by Brother Claver Marlow, who was visiting from Melbourne. By a remarkable coincidence, Brother Marlow had been the principal of St Kevin's College in Melbourne in 1927 when Jimmy Walsh tried to enter the Benedictines at New Norcia and had attended St Kevin's to learn Latin. Brother Marlow instantly recognised Walsh, even though almost thirty years had passed. He knew that Walsh had tried to enter New Norcia by subterfuge and that Fr Little had warned the Benedictines about him. The matter was immediately reported to Cardinal Gilroy of Sydney Diocese, and the decision was taken that Jimmy Walsh would be dismissed from his position.[40]

Correspondence between the Provincial and General of the Christian Brothers show that on 5 September 1953, Brother P.L. Duffy wrote to Brother S.R. Young saying that he had visited Cardinal Gilroy and told him about Kevin Walshe 'the Templemore chap' who was teaching at St Thomas's. His Eminence told Brother Duffy that he would like Brother Claver Marlow to 'have a talk with Police Commissioner Delaney about Walshe.[41] A check-up should be made on the activities of Walshe. His Eminence is rather concerned that

Walshe might be a dangerous type of person to have teaching in one of our Catholic schools.'[42]

Brother Duffy felt that Walsh was a 'danger spot … I would be pleased to hear that he has finished his engagement with us'.[43] On 2 February 1954, Brother Young wrote that he had requested Brother Luke Carey to make enquiries about the history of Jimmy Walsh in Victoria.[44] On 16 February Brother Young wrote that, 'The doings of Walsh in Melbourne brought a negative response as far as police records go.'[45] In November 1954 Walsh was still teaching in St Thomas's, and Brother Duffy wrote to Brother Young asking if there were any cause 'to be concerned about his continuing to teach in one of our schools'.[46] By March 1955 the situation had changed and Jimmy Walsh had been dismissed from his teaching post at St Thomas's. Brother Young wrote that Jimmy Walsh 'received his walking papers at the end of last year and wrote a fierce letter to our First Consultor in which he spoke of Torquemada methods!'.[47] Brother Brian Berg recalled in later life that after Jimmy Walsh was sacked, his son Graydon Bruce, who was a pupil at Saint Ignatius' College, Riverview, came to St Thomas's in uniform to collect his father's final pay packet.[48]

In 1958, after twenty-six years of marriage, Jimmy Walsh issued divorce proceedings against his wife Doris. New South Wales Supreme Court case 1731/1958 was listed as Walshe J.K. versus Walshe D.A.[49] Jimmy gave his address as Birriga Road, Bellvue Hill, and Doris lived at Blaxell Avenue, Granville, both in Sydney.

On 24 June 1958, Jimmy made a statement under oath setting out the reason why he was petitioning to divorce his wife. He stated that the couple had enjoyed a comparatively happy life in the early years of their marriage, but in 1953 he noticed a 'marked cooling off towards me'. When he discussed this with Doris, she said that she no longer loved him and did not want to live with him anymore. He went on to say that in the early months of 1954 Doris started to 'go out dancing every night and also went hiking on weekends'. She left the family home at Leura Road, Double Bay, on 22 June 1954 and never returned.

He finished his statement by saying that he had made many requests of his wife to come back, but on every occasion 'she has refused to return to our home'. Jimmy Walsh stated the reason for requesting a divorce was that Doris had without just cause or excuse 'wilfully deserted him continuously for a three-year period'. He also made a statutory declaration that he had no 'legal obligation to financially support my wife D.A. Walshe'.[50] Doris did not contest the divorce, and on 14 October 1958 a decree nisi giving a date by which the marriage would formally end was issued by Mr Justice Ferguson of the Matrimonial Causes Jurisdiction. The judge issued a ruling, however, that the time for the service of the decree absolute would be abridged to three months 'in view of the petitioner's religious aspirations which are due to commence in February 1959'.[51]

Having been granted a divorce, Jimmy Walsh was making another attempt to join the Sylvestrine Benedictine community at Rydalmere near Sydney, thirty-three years after his failed attempt to join the Benedictines at New Norcia in Western Australia. On 22 August 1959, a letter of reference for Jimmy Walsh was sent to Reverend Father Romauld of the Benedictine order in New South Wales from Franciscan priest Father Benedict O'Donoghue, a missionary based in Aitape, New Guinea. In his letter Father Benedict said that he had come to know Jimmy Walsh very well. Describing him as a 'most exemplary Catholic layman, with a deep faith and a man of great piety', he went on to say that he was most 'docile and humble while at the same time manifesting great strength of character and generosity in his efforts to serve God. He is a truly gentle soul.' Father Benedict expressed his hope that the application would be successful.[52]

On 1 September 1959, Jimmy Walsh was accepted as a 'regular oblate' in the Benedictine order if he were able to 'obtain dispensation from the impediment of being married'. In a vote taken by the monks in Rydalmere, five were in favour and one abstained.[53] Regular oblates generally lived within the community, but were essentially laymen and had no voting rights. On 15 September 1959, Jimmy Walsh's final oblation was received by Fr Romano Cavalieri and he took the name 'Columba' as his oblate name. The monastery archives show that on 13 June 1960, at 8.00 p.m.,

'Mr James Kevin Walshe [*sic*], an Oblate of St Benedict entered our monastery to become a choir monk'.[54] Oblates received the title 'Brother', and on 26 June 1960, 'Brother K. Walshe' was recorded as being present at a meeting of oblates. On 12 September 1960, records show that while Jimmy Walsh had been accepted into the monastery to begin the next phase of his studies for the priesthood, 'the bishop of his native diocese in Ireland refuses to give a testimonial concerning Mr J.K. Walshe. It has been decided to write again to the bishop in order to obtain further clarification of the matter.'[55]

The bishop concerned was Dr Thomas Morris (1914–97), who was appointed as Archbishop of the Diocese of Cashel and Emly in 1960. The story of the Templemore Miracles would have been very well remembered in the diocese, and there were very close Tipperary connections between the hierarchy in Ireland and in Australia, making it very easy for the Australian Church to make enquiries in the county about Jimmy Walsh.

Archbishop O'Donnell of Brisbane came from Fethard in Tipperary and was a close friend of Dr Morris. While in the seminary in Rome training for the priesthood, O'Donnell shared a room with Norman Gilroy, who later became Cardinal Gilroy, and they remained close friends. When O'Donnell was ordained Bishop of Brisbane, the ceremony was carried out by Gilroy, assisted by Bishops Ryan of Sale and Gleeson of Maitland, both of whom also came from Tipperary.

During a visit to Ireland in February 1961 to commemorate the anniversary of the death of Saint Patrick some 1,500 years earlier, Archbishop O'Donnell met an old friend from Fethard, Father Walter Skehan, parish priest of Loughmore/Castleiny, near Templemore. Archbishop O'Donnell related the story of how Jimmy Walsh, 'under an assumed name', had been recognised and reported to the authorities. Archbishop O'Donnell also told Father Skehan that the Benedictines had written to Dr Morris of Cashel and Emly enquiring about Walsh as they were 'about to receive him into their order, even though they knew his history'.[56]

On 10 February 1961, the Benedictine prior of Rydalmere, Fr Cornelius Cornelli, informed a meeting dealing with the issue of Jimmy Walsh's admission to the order that the Congregation for the Religious in Rome had granted an 'indult' of formal permission to J.K. Walshe 'to enter the religious life'. Fr Cornelli recommended the candidate, but when a vote was taken the results were three in favour, two against and two abstained, so the proposal was not carried. Fr Cornelli recommended that another meeting take place when two priests who were away studying at the archdiocesan seminary in Manly returned, and another vote could be taken.[57] While Fr Cornelli was keen to have Jimmy Walsh join the monastery, other monks saw difficulties given that he was divorced and that during those proceedings Walsh had stated publically that he 'had to get divorced in order to become a monk'. Cardinal Gilroy was 'not at all pleased by this publicity, and told the monks so!' Father Alberic Jacovone of Rydalmere, who knew Jimmy Walsh personally, recalled in later life the 'displeasure of Cardinal Gilroy' over this incident.[58]

Despite the fact that Walsh had been sacked from his position as a teacher by the Roman Catholic Church in 1955 when he was recognised by Brother Claver Marlow, he had secured a position as one of three lay teachers in the boys' primary school attached to the monastery at Rydalmere. The school had been established at the request of Cardinal Gilroy in 1958 but closed in 1960. Father Giovanni Messore of Rydalmere remembered Jimmy Walsh as a middle-aged man who 'kindly gave him English lessons' when he arrived from Italy knowing very little of the language.[59] Father Messore also recalled that when Jimmy Walsh won a transistor radio in a school raffle, he gave it to the priest so that he could listen to radio programmes to improve his English, including one called *English for migrants*. Another recollection of Father Messore was that Walsh frequently complained of headaches when he knew him, and he took a popular medicine called Bex Powders, which used the advertising tagline 'A cup of tea, a Bex and a good lie down'. Bex was recommended for headaches, colds and flu, all nerve pains, rheumatism and for 'calming down the overexcited'. It was withdrawn from use in 1983 due to its damaging action on the kidneys and carcinogenic properties.

In April 1961 another vote was held regarding Walsh's admission to the Benedictines, and on this occasion the results were four in favour, three against and one abstained. As there was not a majority in favour, the proposal was lost for a second time.[60] That was not the end of the matter, however, and in November 1961 Jimmy Walsh received a letter from Father O'Donoghue in New Guinea, who had written a letter of reference for Jimmy Walsh in 1959. O'Donoghue wrote that he was 'delighted to learn that at long last the door has been opened for you to set out for the attainment of your noble resolve'. He also referred to 'conditions set down by the cardinal' which would be 'a set back to you for a start. It means the breaking of many ties that are very dear to you. But, if our Lord asks such things of you, you can be sure that He will give you the grace to do them for Him.'

The conditions imposed by the cardinal are not specified, but plans had been finalised by the Benedictines in Rydalmere to send Jimmy Walsh to Oxford, Michigan, some 30 miles from Detroit in the USA, to enter the Saint Sylvester Benedictine Monastery. Given the controversy which surrounded Walsh, perhaps Cardinal Gilroy had decided that he could only become a monk if it were in another country. This would explain the reference to the 'breaking of ties that are very dear to you'. Ending his letter, Father O'Donoghue told Walsh that their paths would 'probably not cross again, however I will be thinking of you and praying for you,

Kevin … thanking you for your many kindnesses and your generosity to me over the years'.[61]

Writing to the American Consul in Sydney on 7 June 1962 on behalf of the Benedictine order, the American Travel Company of Sydney stated that they:

> took pleasure in introducing Mr J.K. Walshe of Murriverie Road, North Bondi, who departs Sydney on Thursday next for Detroit where he has been accepted as candidate in the religious order at St Sylvester Monastery. Mr Walshe will present supporting documents to complete his application for a US Visa. Transportation has been provided from Sydney to Detroit via San Francisco, one way.[62]

There is no evidence that Jimmy Walsh ever made the journey to the USA to begin a canonical novitiate to prepare him for the priesthood. He did not continue to teach, and at the time of his death his occupation was listed as 'wardsman', which is a hospital porter/healthcare assistant. In the early 1970s Jimmy Walsh's health began to deteriorate when he suffered a serious injury after being hit by a car. He became resident in a nursing home in Fairfield, and family members recall that he liked to hear them sing songs such as 'Irish eyes are smiling' and 'Danny boy' to him. Even though he had lost most of his ability to talk, he would smile and become emotional when he heard such reminders of Ireland. Father Messore of the Benedictines, who knew Jimmy well from his time in the monastery at Rydalmere, visited him regulary in the nursing home and recalled that he was 'shaking all of the time'.[63]

Even though they had divorced in 1958 in acrimonious circumstances, Doris remarried Jimmy on 6 July 1973 at Guildford Heights Private Hospital (now the Holroyd Private Hospital) in Sydney. The marriage was a civil ceremony performed under the rites of the Roman Catholic Church, and was witnessed by Elisabeth McKinnon (née Walshe), Jimmy and Doris's daughter. James Kevin Walsh died on 12 March 1977 at Auburn Hospital in Sydney. The cause of death was given as 'cardiac arrest, pneumonia and mitral valve disease'. He was buried on 16 March in the Roman Catholic plot in Pine Grove Memorial Park, Minchinbury, Sydney. The funeral service was carried out by Father Alberic Jacovone of the Benedictines, who knew Jimmy Walsh from his days at Rydalmere.[64]

Doris Ada Walshe died in 2000 and was predeceased by her son Graydon Bruce, who lived with Doris until his premature death in 1993 aged only 52. Graydon Kevin Walshe had died at birth in 1939. Isobel Margaret Ann Walshe was born in 1933, became a medical doctor and married Russell Kippax. They had three children: Ruth, Pauline and Rodney. Elizabeth Mary Kathleen Walshe, born in 1937, married Ronald Douglas McKinnon. They also had three children: Robert, Susan and Margaret.

Conclusion

''Tis mad idolatry to make the service greater than
the God.'

William Shakespeare[1]

The story of the so-called Templemore Miracles, or
bleeding statues, has fascinated, intrigued and amused
people in equal measure for decades. Similar events
were reported in the small town of Ballinspittle, County
Cork, in 1985, and as had happened in Templemore
over fifty years earlier, hundreds of thousands of people
visited the town in the space of a few weeks. Most came
to pray, while others came out of curiosity or merely
to gaze at the ongoing spectacle. Bishop Michael
Murphy of the Diocese of Cork and Ross dismissed
events in Ballinspittle as an optical illusion, and urged
caution. Eventually, as had taken place in Templemore
and Curraheen, the pilgrims stopped coming. The
shrine in Ballinspittle remains today, is lovingly tended

to and is still visited by many pilgrims each year. In Templemore and Curraheen, however, nothing stands as a reminder of the extraordinary events which took place in August and September 1920. The phenomenon of Marian apparition or moving and bleeding statues has also entered popular culture in Ireland. For example, in his book *A Star Called Henry*, first published in 2000, the best-selling Irish author Roddy Doyle dramatised events in Templemore, describing the alleged visionary Jimmy Walsh as a 'wee priest-to-be, a seminarian, home on his holidays, being fattened by his mammy for winter'.[2]

The phenomenon of the Templemore Miracles briefly transformed a small rural community into a place of pilgrimage and hope for tens of thousands of people, not only from Ireland but from overseas. The miracles took place at a time of desperation when a bitter and divisive conflict was raging in Ireland. Simple people took refuge in their faith, many of them believing that divine intervention had occurred to prevent further violence and bloodshed. While this book was not about religion as such, the research suggests that the miracles and apparitions were not genuine and appear to have been the work of a misguided individual or individuals who engineered them for their own reasons. The exact reason may remain a mystery, as James Walsh left Ireland shortly afterwards, never to return, but there are several possibilities which merit consideration. Walsh's brother was a Republican hunger striker in jail in England at the time of the miracles, so perhaps his intention was to assist the Republican cause by raising funds or causing a distraction for the military and police. Perhaps Walsh genuinely believed that he was experiencing Marian visions. It is equally possible that he sought money, fame and publicity, which he certainly obtained, if only for a brief period. The possibility also exists that James Walsh was manipulated by others for their own purposes. When Michael Collins broke open one of the statues and examined it, the sophisticated mechanism found inside suggests that the hoax was an elaborate one, which may have involved several persons.

The fact that Collins ordered Commandant Séan Harling to travel to Tipperary and return with one of the statues for examination demonstrates how seriously the Republican leadership viewed the situation, and that the hoax was not organised or approved at that level. The IRA exploited the miracles for their own military and economic reasons. While benefiting from the situation, however, they simultaneously pressurised the Catholic Church to denounce the miracles. When this pressure was rebuffed by the Church, the IRA took brutal and decisive action to bring the period of the miracles to an end following the interrogation of the alleged visionary Jimmy Walsh.

As with many other Marian apparitions which have occurred throughout the ages, a lack of endorsement by the Catholic Church would have ensured that the religious fervour surrounding the Templemore Miracles would eventually peter out, but the IRA took pre-emptive action instead. In doing so they crossed a boundary between religion and politics. Walsh was brought to Dublin and interrogated by Dan Breen at the behest of Michael Collins, and was doubtless fortunate to escape the fate of so many others who were suspected of being spies, informers or otherwise being an 'enemy of the republic'. It is perhaps no coincidence that he left Ireland for Australia shortly after the miracles. During the Kiloskehan ambush the IRA coldly and calculatedly killed two policemen, knowing that this act was liable to elicit a savage reprisal by the police and military, as had happened so often in the past during the conflict. The fear of reprisals for this ambush drove pilgrims from Templemore and Curraheen, never to return, and the Templemore Miracles ended as suddenly as they had begun.

When the war resumed in earnest, it was fought with an intensity and ferocity which had not previously been seen. The reality of the war was far removed from the romantic version of events espoused by Republicans like Dan Breen in his autobiography *My fight for Irish freedom*. The RIC was gradually withdrawn from rural areas as the conflict escalated, and the IRA usurped many of their functions. Republican courts and Republican police operated with relative impunity, and no one dared openly assist the forces of law and order. The IRA exerted its self-appointed authority over the local population, imposing its own martial law, and 'the boys' acted as judge, jury and executioner. The IRA had a huge advantage over British forces as it exercised a psychological dominance over the Irish people and had inherited the mantle of the old agrarian secret societies such as the Ribbonmen.

Atrocities were committed by both sides, and the police and military fell into the trap skilfully set for them by the IRA by engaging in reprisal attacks. Such actions provoked huge criticism in England and around the world. In Templemore neither set of combatants emerged from the conflict morally untainted, although with the passage of time events have become sanitised and the indefensible has become defensible. Research suggests that Templemore was much more prosperous under British rule than as part of the Irish Free State. As a garrison town it was largely dependent on Richmond Barracks for prosperity, and when the British withdrew the barracks effectively closed down. In common with other garrison towns, the local population had a close social and economic relationship with the barracks and a huge void was left when the soldiers marched out for the last time. On 9 December 1921, *The Irish Times* predicted that the withdrawal of the military from the garrison towns of Ireland would be a 'source of profound regret' and that the loss of trade generated by the army to towns 'which owed the greater part of their trade to the military…would now be hard hit unless some compensating factor is supplied'.[3] Decades passed before Templemore became prosperous again.

It remains a mystery exactly how and why Jimmy Walsh went to Australia, but he had become an embarrassment to both the IRA and the Catholic Church. Having been labelled a suspected spy by Dan Breen, Walsh was liable to be executed, but he was only 16 years old and many people believed that he was a genuine visionary. His emigration from Ireland thus solved the problem for the IRA over what to do with him. The Catholic Church may also have had a role, as many of the Australian hierarchy were Irish. Archbishop Clune visited Templemore during the period of the miracles and told the local IRA that members of the RIC who resigned for moral or ethical reasons would be given safe passage and assistance in gaining employment when they arrived in Australia. The Church provided a conduit between Ireland and Australia for those who needed to relocate because of the situation in Ireland, so the possibility exists that this channel was used in the case of Jimmy Walsh.[4]

Walsh never returned to Ireland, and people who enquired about him were told that he had died in Australia, decades before his actual death. This had the effect of preventing awkward questions from being asked. The reality of his life in Australia is as captivating as his previous life in Ireland. After emigrating he altered his name, got married in 1932 and had three children. In later life, however, his true identity was revealed, which brought profound consequences. He was dismissed from his job as a lay teacher at the behest of the Catholic Church, but despite this setback he later tried repeatedly, but ultimately unsuccessfully, to join a religious order.

Walsh shares many of the characteristics of others over the centuries who have alleged that they experienced Marian apparitions or that icons or statues wept tears of blood. They are generally young people from humble rural backgrounds who have shown strong religious devotion prior to claiming that they were experiencing visions. Many have also been involved in religious practices such as pilgrimages, devotions, processions and prayers, which has been defined as 'popular piety'.[5] In 1974 Pope Paul VI, writing in *Evangelii nuntiandi* (article 48), said that such piety 'indicates a certain thirst for God such as only those who are simple and poor in spirit can experience. ... It can bear such excellent fruits and yet is fraught with danger.'[6] This danger manifested itself in the extraordinary story of James Kevin Walsh and the Templemore Miracles of 1920.

NOTES

Chapter 1

1   Loft, Martin, *Harry Loft and the 64th Regiment of Foot* (Staffordshire: 2003), p.64.

2   *Saunder's News-letter,* 11 November 1808.

3   Costello, Con, *A Most Delightful Station* (Dublin: 1996), p.21.

4   May, Trevor, *Military Barracks* (Buckinghamshire: 2002), p.8.

5   Costello, *A Most Delightful Station*, p.23.

6   Gash, Norman, *Mr Secretary Peel: the Life of Sir Robert Peel to 1830* (New York: 1971), quoted in Broeker, Galen, *Rural Disorder and Police Reform in Ireland 1812–36* (London: 1970), p.36; also Hurd, Douglas, *Sir Robert Peel: A Biography* (London: 2007), p.36.

7   *Ibid*.

8   Peel to Abbot, 25 December 1816, in Peel Private papers, i, 236, quoted in Broeker, Galen, *Rural Disorder and Police Reform in Ireland in Ireland 1812–36* (London: 1970), p.25.

9   Letter from E.B. Littlehales to Mother Clare Ursula, 10 November 1804; Ursuline Archives, Thurles.

10 Borrow, George, *Levengro* (London: 1893), p.51.

11 Lewis, Samuel, *A Topographical Dictionary of Ireland, Part II* (Dublin: 1837), Vol.II–609, p.41.

12   Bartlett, Thomas and Jeffrey, Keith, *A Military History of Ireland* (Cambridge: 1996), p.337.

13   *Ibid.*

14   *Tipperary Vindicator*, 16 November 1844.

15   *Leinster Express*, 1 December 1855.

16   *All the Year Round*, 26 November 1864, Volume XII, p.370 (http://www.djo.org.uk/all-the-year-round/volume-xii/page-370.html: accessed 17 July 2017).

17   Loft, M., *Harry Loft and the 64th Regiment of Foot*, p.64.

18   *Nenagh Guardian*, 14 May 1857.

19   Letter from the War Office to Templemore Urban District Council, 25 January 1909 (United Kingdom National Archives T1/11376).

20   Nevinson, Henry, 'Sir Roger Casement and Sinn Féin', *Atlantic Magazine*, 2 February 1916. Quoted in Holt, Edgar, *Protest in Arms, the Irish Troubles 1916–1923* (New York: 1960), p.101.

21   *Tipperary Star*, 6 May 1916.

22   Ryan, Desmond, *Seán Treacy and the Third Tipperary Brigade* (Tralee: 1945), p.23.

23   Statement of Dan Breen, Bureau of Military History, witness statement 1739, p.19 (hereafter BMH/WS).

24   Augusteijn, Joost, *From Public Defiance to Guerrilla Warfare* (London: 1996), p.55.

25   Statement of Edward McGrath, BMH/WS 1522, p.4.

26   Townshend, Charles, *The British Military Campaign in Ireland 1919–1921, the Development of Political and Military Policies* (Oxford: 1975), p.7.

27   Seán Gaynor, 'With Tipperary No. 1 Brigade in North Tipperary 1917–21, Part 1' in *Tipperary Historical Journal* (1993), p. 32.

28   Note on the IRA and the South Tipperary Brigade. University College Dublin, Mulcahy papers, P7b/181; quoted in Hopkinson, Michael, *The Irish War of Independence* (Dublin: 2002), p.117.

29   Statement of Dan Breen, BMH/WS 1739, p.24.

30   Kee, Robert, *Ireland, A History* (London: 1980), p.180.

31 Augusteijn, *From Public Defiance to Guerrilla Warfare*, p.83.

32 *Ibid.*, p.18.

33 Ryan, *Seán Treacy and the Third Tipperary Brigade,* p.56.

34 Statement of Edward McGrath, BMH/WS 1522, p.7.

35 RIC Inspector General's monthly report, July 1920, NAI. CO 904/112.

36 *Ibid.*

37 *Tipperary Star*, 21 August 1920.

38 Herlihy, James, *Royal Irish Constabulary Officers, a Biographical Dictionary and Genealogical Guide, 1816–1922* (Dublin: 2005), p.171.

39 Gaynor, 'With Tipperary No. 1 Brigade in North Tipperary 1917–21, Part 1', in *Tipperary Historical Journal* (1993), p.34.

40 Statement of Patrick Kinnane, BMH/WS 1475, p.10.

41 Statement of James Leahy, BMH/WS 1454, p.18.

42 *Irish Independent*, 24 June 1919.

43 *Irish Independent*, 25 June 1919.

44 Statement of James Leahy, BMH/WS 1454, p.19.

45 *Irish Independent*, 25 June 1919.

46 RIC County Inspector's monthly report, June 1919, NAI. CO 904/109.

47 *Irish Independent*, 25 June 1919.

48 RIC County Inspector's monthly report, June 1919, NAI. CO 904/109.

49 *Irish Independent*, 30 June 1919.

50 *Ibid.*

51 Lord John French served as Lord Lieutenant of Ireland from 1918–21. He survived a number of assassination attempts, including the Ashtown incident of December 1919, and proclaimed martial law on 10 December 1920. He was named by a coroner's jury as being responsible for the death of Mayor Thomas MacCurtain of Cork. See *Who's Who in the Irish War of Independence 1916–1920* (Oxford: 1975), p.26.

52 *Irish Times*, 26 January 1920.

53 Statement of James Leahy, BMH/WS 1454, p.35.

54   Statement of Edward McGrath, BMH/WS 1522, p.10.
55   *Freemans Journal*, 18 August 1920.
56   Statement of James Leahy, BMH/WS 1454, p.35.
57   Statement of Michael Hynes, BMH/WS 1671, p.3.
58   Statement of James Leahy, BMH/WS 1454, p.19.
59   *Freemans Journal*, 18 August 1920.
60   *Ibid.*
61   RIC County Inspector,s report, Tipperary North Riding, August 1920, NAI.CO 904/112.
62   *Ibid.*
63   *Tipperary Star*, 19 August 1920.
64   Letter of Rev. W.T. Cairns to the Wilson family, August 1920. Wilson family archive, reproduced with the permission of Ms Stephanie Sims.
65   *Irish Times*, 18 August 1920.
66   *Irish Independent*, 20 August 1920.
67   *Irish Examiner*, 28 October 1920.
68   Gurney, Russell, *History of the Northamptonshire Regiment 1742–1934*, p.153.
69   Townsend, *The British Military Campaign in Ireland 1919–1921*, p.53.
70   Gurney, *History of the Northamptonshire Regiment*, p.340.
71   *Tipperary Star*, 21 August 1920.
72   RIC County Inspector's report, Tipperary North Riding, January 1920, NAI.CO 904/112.
73   Hopkinson, *The Irish War of Independence,* p.80.
74   *Anglo-Celt*, 21 August 1920.
75   *Irish Independent*, 20 August 1920.
76   *Thom's Official Directory of the United Kingdom of Great Britain and Ireland, 1920* (Dublin: 1910), p.1358.
77   *The London Gazette*, 25 August 1917.
78   Operational diary of the Northamptonshire Regiment in Ireland, 1919–23, Northampton County Archives.
79   *Irish Times*, 12 November 1920.
80   *Northampton Daily Chronicle*, 21 August 1920.
81   *Tipperary Star*, 21 August 1920.
82   *Freemans Journal*, 18 August 1920.

83 Paddy Kinnane, 'My part in the war of independence, part II', in *Tipperary Historical Journal* (1996), p.103.

84 Statement of James Duggan, BMH/WS 1510, p.15.

85 *Freemans Journal,* 21 August 1920.

86 Statement of James Leahy, BMH/WS 1454, p.38.

87 *Ibid.*

88 Hopkinson, *The Irish War of Independence*, p.127.

89 Street, C.J.C., *The Administration of Ireland, 1920* (London: 1921), p.147.

90 *Ibid.*, p.148.

91 Mulcahy, Risteárd, *My Father, the General, Richard Mulcahy and the Military History of the Revolution* (Dublin: 2009), p.52.

92 RIC Inspector General's monthly report, August 1920, NAI.CO 904/109.

93 Gurney, *History of the Northamptonshire Regiment*, p.340.

94 *Irish Times,* 6 September 1920.

Chapter 2

1 *Irish Times*, 23 August 1920.

2 *Ibid.*

3 Martin, Hugh, *Ireland in Insurrection, an Englishman's Record of Fact* (London: 1921), p.98.

4 *Freemans Journal* (Sydney), 4 November 1920.

5 *Ibid.*

6 *Ibid.*

7 *Tipperary Star*, 20 August 1920.

8 *Limerick Leader*, 3 September 1920.

9 *Ibid.*

10 RIC County Inspector's report, Tipperary North Riding, August 1920, NAI.CO 904/112.

11 *Tipperary Star*, 4 September 1920.

12 *Tipperary Star*, 20 August, 1920.

13 *Tipperary Star*, 16 August 1920.

14 *Tipperary Star*, 4 September 1920.

15   RIC general register, NAI.HO 184.

16   Fitzpatrick, David, *Politics and Irish Life 1913–1921, Provincial Experiences of War and Revolution* (Cork: 1977), p.33.

17   *Tipperary Star*, 20 March 1920.

18   *An t-Óglách*, 1 May 1920.

19   See *The Nation* (London), 10 January 1920, also the *Daily Mail*, 3 April 1920, quoted in Macardle, Dorothy, *The Irish Republic* (London: 1937), p.340.

20   Holt, Edgar, *Protest in Arms, the Irish Troubles 1916–1923* (New York: 1960), p.201. William O'Brien (1852–1928), Member of Parliament for Mallow, was proprietor of the *Cork Free Press* and a renowned orator. He was a leading member of the All for Ireland League that preached 'conference, conciliation and consent'. See O'Farrell, Padraic, *Who's Who in the Irish War of Independence 1916–1921* (Dublin: 1980), p.119.

21   Shea, Patrick, *Voices and the Sound of Drums, an Irish Autobiography* (Belfast: 1981), p.45.

22   *Ibid.*

23   Street, *The Administration of Ireland*, p.276.

24   *Limerick Leader*, 20 September 1920.

25   RIC County Inspector's report, Tipperary North Riding, August 1920, NAI.CO 904/112.

26   *Irish Independent*, 31 August 1920.

27   *Irish Independent*, 2 September 1920.

28   Correspondence between the author and Mr John O'Grady, Clongour, Thurles, 28 June 2016.

29   *Irish Times*, 23 August 1920.

30   Interview with William O'Meara, Templemore, 16 March 2006. Author's collection.

31   *Limerick Leader*, 4 September 1920.

32   *New York Times*, 22 August 1920.

33   Martin, *Ireland in Insurrection, an Englishman's Record of Fact*, p.98.

34   *Ibid.*, p.96.

35   *Ibid.*, p.98.

36   *Irish Independent,* 4 September 1920.

37   *Ocean Evening Herald* (New York), 31 August 1920.

38   *Daily Mirror,* 24 August 1920.

39   *Ibid.*

40   *Nenagh Guardian,* 28 August 1920.

41   *Evening Herald,* 23 August 1920.

42   *Nenagh News,* 28 August 1920.

43   *Tipperary Star,* 20 August 1920. Note: there is no record of James Walsh ever having been a member or a novice in the Cistercian order.

44   *Rockhampton Morning Bulletin* (Queensland), 15 November 1920.

45   *Limerick Leader,* 23 August 1920.

46   *Irish Times,* 23 August 1920.

47   *Ibid.*

48   *Ibid.*

49   Holy wells were commonplace in Ireland, with over 30,000 recorded locations. Quoted in Harbinson, Peter, *Pilgrimage in Ireland, the Monuments and the People* (London: 1991), p.229.

50   *Tipperary Star,* 20 August 1920.

51   *Freemans Journal* (Sydney), 4 November 1920.

52   Harbinson, *Pilgrimage in Ireland, the Monuments and the People,* p.230.

53   *Tipperary Star,* 4 September 1920.

54   *Tipperary Star,* 11 September 1920.

55   Martin, *Ireland in Insurrection, an Englishman's Record of Fact,* p.101.

56   *Tipperary Star,* 18 September 1920.

57   *Irish Examiner,* 27 August 1920.

58   *Ogden Standard Examiner* (Utah), 26 August 1920.

59   *Tipperary Star,* 4 September 1920.

60   *Ibid.*

61   *Tipperary Star,* 18 September 1920.

62   *Tipperary Star,* 30 August 1920.

63   *Ibid.*

64   *Limerick Leader,* 28 August 1920.

65 *Freemans Journal* (Sydney), 4 November 1920.

66 Shea, *Voices and the Sound of Drums, an Irish Autobiography*, p.49.

67 *Ibid.*

68 *Ibid.*

69 Martin, *Ireland in Insurrection, an Englishman's Record of Fact*, p.100.

70 *Ibid.*

71 *Irish Examiner*, 27 August 1920.

72 *Tipperary Star*, 4 September 1920.

73 *Adelaide Southern Cross*, 28 January 1921.

74 'Miracle', *Merriam-Webster Dictionary* (https://www.mer-riam-webster.com: last accessed 4 October 2019).

75 Nickel, Joseph, *Looking for a Miracle, Weeping Icons, Relics, Stigmata, Visions and Healing Cures* (New York: 1993), p.9.

76 Donnelly, James, 'The revival of Knock shrine', in *History and the Public Sphere, Essays in Honour of John A. Murphy* (Cork: 2004), p.187.

77 *Irish Times*, 23 August 1920.

78 *Limerick Leader*, 13 September 1920.

79 *Freemans Journal*, 23 August 1920, see also *Tipperary Star*, 30 August 1920.

80 Skehan papers, *Index of Clergy of the Archdiocese of Cashel and Emly*, Vol. 4, p.84. Cashel and Emly Diocesan Archives, Thurles.

81 *Skibbereen Eagle*, 28 August 1920.

82 Correspondence between the author and John O'Grady, Clongour, Thurles, 28 June 2016.

83 *Irish Times*, 11 September 1920.

84 *Irish Times*, 13 September 1920.

85 *Ibid.*

86 *Ibid.*

87 *Meath Chronicle*, 2 October 1920.

88 *Ibid.*

89 Dwyer, T.R., *Big Fellow, Long fellow, a Joint Biography of Collins and De Valera* (Dublin: 1999), p.146.

90 *Western Australia Record*, 27 November 1920.

91 *Irish Times*, 27 December 1920.

92 *Irish Times*, 7 September 1920.

93 *Ibid*.

94 Statement of James Leahy, BMH/WS 1454, p.44.

95 Statement of Liam Hoolan, BMH/WS 1553, p.16.

96 Statement of James Leahy, BMH/WS 1454, p.43.

97 Statement of Edward McGrath, BMH/WS 1522, p.14.

98 *Rockhampton Morning Bulletin* (Queensland), 15 November 1920.

99 *Limerick Leader*, 3 September 1920.

100 *Tipperary Star*, 18 September 1920.

101 *Nenagh Guardian*, 18 December 1920.

102 Statement of Tomas O'Maoileoin, BMH/WS 845, p.93.

103 *Nationalist and Leinster Times*, 23 October, 1920.

104 *Ibid*.

105 *The Irish Catholic,* 16 October 1920.

106 *Nationalist and Leinster Times,* 23 October 1920.

107 *The Irish Catholic*, 16 October 1920.

108 *Ibid*.

109 *Tipperary Star*, 4 September 1920.

110 Statement of Edward McGrath, BMH/WS 1522, p.14.

111 *Ibid*., p.15.

112 Statement of James Duggan, BMH/WS 1510, p.17.

113 *Limerick Leader*, 3 September 1920.

114 Statement of James Duggan, BMH/WS 1510, p.16.

115 *Tipperary Star*, 4 September 1920.

116 Statement of James Leahy, BMH/WS 1454, p.44.

117 *Ibid*., p.42.

118 *Ibid*., p.43.

119 *Ibid*., p.44.

120 Statement of Séamus Robinson, BMH/WS 1721, p.123.

121 *Ibid*.

122 Statement of Colonel Joseph Lawless, BMH/WS 1043, p.323.

123 Statement of Dan Breen, BMH/WS 1739, p.36.

124 Hart, Peter, *Mick: The Real Michael Collins* (London: 2005), p.71.

125 Statement of Dan Breen, BMH/WS 1739, p.37.

126   *Ibid.*
127   *Ibid.*, p.112.
128   *Ibid.*, p.36.

Chapter 3

1   *Nenagh Guardian*, 22 January 1921.
2   Abbott, Richard, *Police Casualties in Ireland, 1919–22*
      (Dublin: 2000), p.127.
3   Statement of James Leahy, BMH/WS 1454, p.42.
4   RIC County Inspector's report, Tipperary North Riding,
      November 1920, NAI.CO 904/112.
5   Statement of James Leahy, BMH/WS 1454, p.42.
6   *Ibid.*
7   *Ibid.*
8   *Nenagh Guardian*, 22 January 1921.
9   *Ibid.*
10   Griffith, Kenneth and O'Grady, Timothy, *Curious Journey, an
      Oral History of Ireland's Unfinished Revolution* (Dublin: 1998),
      pp.158–9.
11   *Ibid.*
12   Statement of Daniel Kelly, BMH/WS 1004, p.16.
13   Statement of James Kilmartin, BMH/WS 881, p.8.
14   The operational diary of the Northamptonshire Regiment
      records that a certificate for 'gallant conduct' during the
      Thomastown ambush was awarded to a Corporal Goode
      from the 1st Battalion.
15   *Irish Times*, 30 October 1920.
16   *Northampton Mercury*, 5 November 1920.
17   *Tipperary Star*, 6 November 1920.
18   *Irish Independent*, 1 November 1920.
19   *Irish Independent*, 2 November 1920.
20   *Evening Herald*, 1 November 1920.
21   RIC County Inspector's report, Tipperary North Riding,
      December 1920, NAI.CO 904/112.
22   *Freemans Journal*, 1 November 1920.

23 *Ibid*.
24 *Tipperary Star*, 1 November 1920.
25 *Irish Independent*, 2 November 1920.
26 Statement of Edward McGrath, BMH/WS 1522, p.18.
27 *The Times*, 20 September 1920.
28 *Nenagh Guardian*, 22 January 1921.
29 RIC Inspector General's monthly report, September 1920, NAI.CO 904/110.
30 *Ibid*.
31 Martin, *Ireland in Insurrection, an Englishman's Record of Fact*, p.105.
32 *Appleton Post Crescent* (Wisconsin), 14 September 1920.
33 Statement of Seán Gaynor, BMH/WS 1389, p.12.
34 Statement of Edward O'Leary, BMH/WS 1459, p.12.
35 Statement of Edward Ryan, BMH/WS 1392, p.8.
36 Gurney, *History of the Northamptonshire Regiment*, p.340.
37 Statement of Liam Hoolan, BMH/WS 1553, p.9.
38 *Irish Times*, 8 November 1920.
38 *Ibid*.
39 Statement of Con Spain, BMH/WS 1464, p.8.
40 *The Times*, 10 November 1920.
41 *Ibid*.
42 Statement of Edward McGrath, BMH/WS 1522, p.27.
43 *Irish Times*, 6 November 1920.
44 *Western Morning Post*, 12 November 1920.
45 Statement of Edward McGrath, BMH/WS 1522, p.27.
46 RIC County Inspector's report, Tipperary North Riding, December 1920, NAI.CO 904/112.
47 Statement of Edward McGrath, BMH/WS 1522, p.28.
48 *Ibid*., p.29.
49 *Tipperary Star*, 23 October 1920.
50 A Copeswoodian, *Copeswood, 75 Years of Service* (Pallaskenry: 1994), p.20.
51 *1901 Census of Ireland*, Tipperary County, Templemore District Electoral Division, household no. 14 Georges Street. National Archives of Ireland (http://www.census.national-archives.ie: accessed 20 March 2017).

52 A Copeswoodian, *Copeswood, 75 Years of Service*, p.21.

53 *Freeman's Journal* (Sydney), 18 November 1920.

54 *Southern Cross* (Adelaide), 5 November 1920.

55 *Freeman's Journal* (Sydney), 18 November 1920.

56 Nanikivell Loch, Joice, *Ireland in Travail* (London: 1932), p.73.

57 *Nenagh Guardian*, 11 December 1920.

58 *1911 Census of Ireland*, Tipperary County, Thurles Urban District Electoral Division, household no. 161 Pudding Lane. National Archives of Ireland (http://www.census. nationalarchives.ie: accessed 20 March 2017).

59 RIC Inspector General's monthly reports, July and August 1920, NAI.CO 904/112.

60 Statement of James Leahy, BMH/WS 1454, p.77.

61 *Ibid.*, p.78.

62 *Nenagh Guardian*, 2 July 1921.

63 RIC County Inspector's report, Tipperary North Riding, February 1921, NAI.CO 904/114.

64 *Ibid.*

65 Abbott, *Police Casualties in Ireland, 1919–22*, p.285.

66 *Irish Independent*, 1 July 1921.

67 *Irish Times*, 18 August 1921.

68 *Ibid.*

69 Weekly Survey of the State of Ireland, November 1921, National Archives CAB/24/131.

70 *Ibid.*

71 Memo from RIC Deputy Inspector General Walsh to all county and district inspectors, 9 December 1921, NAI.CO 904/178.

72 RIC County Inspector's report, Tipperary North Riding, August 1921, NAI.CO 904/116.

73 *Irish Times*, 13 April 1922.

74 *Irish Independent*, 11 May 1922.

75 *Irish Times*, 9 December 1921.

76 *Northamptonshire Regimental Diary*, 1919–23, p.341.

77 Gurney, *History of the Northamptonshire Regiment*, p.341.

78 *Irish Times*, 1 February 1922.

79   *Nenagh Guardian*, 25 February 1922.
80   Correspondence between the author and John O'Grady, Clongour, Thurles, 28 June 2016.
81   *Ibid.*, 2 January 2017.

Chapter 4

1   Letter from Father T.J. Little to the Abbott of New Norcia, 23 February 1925, New Norcia Archives Reference 01596.

2   Passenger manifest for the steamship *Ormuz*, 31 March 1922, UK National Archives (http://www.nationalarchives. gov.uk: accessed 21 March 2017).

3   O'Donoghue, Kathleen, 'Brady, John (1800–1871)', *Australian Dictionary of Biography, National Centre of Biography*, Australian National University (http://adb.anu.edu.au/ biography/brady-john-1821/text2087, published first in hardcopy 1966, accessed online 27 December 2017).

4   Letter from Father T.J. Little to the Abbott of New Norcia, 23 February 1925, New Norcia Archives Reference 01596.

5   *Ibid.*

6   Correspondence between the author and the Salvation Army International Heritage Centre, William Booth College, London, 3 January 2018.

7   Correspondence between the author and the Uniting Church in Western Australia, Perth, 22 January 2018.

8   Letter from Father T.J. Little to the Abbott of New Norcia, 8 April 1925, New Norcia Archives Reference 01596.

9   Letter from Reverend Castanares to Father T.J. Little, 13 April 1925, New Norcia Archives Reference 01596.

10   Letter from Father T.J. Little to Reverend Castanares, 21 April 1925, New Norcia Archives Reference 01596.

11   Letter from Brother William to New Norcia, 25 July 1925, New Norcia Archives Reference 01596.

12   Letter from Father T.J. Little to Reverend Castanares, 11 August 1925, New Norcia Archives Reference 01596.

13   Letter from Father T.J. Little to Dom Catalan, 1 January 1926, New Norcia Archives Reference 01596.

14   Letter from Father T.J. Little to Dom Catalan, 9 February 1926, New Norcia Archives Reference 01596.

15   Letter from Jimmy Walsh to Dom Catalan, 12 February 1926, New Norcia Archives Reference 01596.

16   Baptismal certificate of James Walsh, 4 February 1959, Walsh family papers.

17   Letter from Jimmy Walsh to Dom Catalan, 6 October 1926, New Norcia Archives Reference 01596.

18   Daniel Mannix came from Charleville in County Cork and was appointed Archbishop of Melbourne Diocese in 1912. An opponent of conscription and strong advocate for Irish independence, he was refused entry to Ireland by the British government in 1920 while travelling from the USA to Rome. His ship was boarded off the Cork coast and he was landed instead at Penzance, causing Mannix to quip that it was 'the greatest victory the Royal Navy has had since Jutland, without the loss of a single British sailor'. The incident made Prime Minister Lloyd George look foolish and portrayed Mannix as a victim. Forbidden to visit Liverpool, Manchester or Glasgow because of their large Irish populations, he drew huge crowds outside their environs and throughout England and Scotland. Griffin, James, 'Mannix, Daniel (1864–1963)', *Australian Dictionary of Biography, National Centre of Biography*, Australian National University (http://adb.anu.edu.au/biography/mannix-daniel-7478/text13033, published first in hardcopy 1986, accessed online 28 December 2017). See also O'Farrell, Padraic, *Who's Who in the Irish War of Independence 1916–1921* (Dublin: 1980), p.107.

19   Letter from Jimmy Walsh to Dom Catalan, 12 November 1926, New Norcia Archives Reference 01596.

20   Letter from Jimmy Walsh to Dom Catalan, 7 January 1927, New Norcia Archives Reference 01596.

21   Letter from Jimmy Walsh to Dom Catalan, 24 January 1927, New Norcia Archives Reference 01596.

22 Letter from Jimmy Walsh to Dom Catalan, 24 August 1927, New Norcia Archives Reference 01596.

23 Letter from Father T.J. Little to Dom Catalan, 5 December 1927, New Norcia Archives Reference 01596.

24 *Moore Theological College Register of Students*, 14 June 1929, p.528, Moore College Archives, Sydney.

25 Letter from Reverend John Bidwell, 8 April 1929, Moore College Archives, Sydney.

26 Mitchell, Bruce, 'Kilgour, Alexander James (1861–1944)', *Australian Dictionary of Biography* (http://adb.anu.edu.au/biography/kilgour-alexander-james-6954/text12077: last accessed 4 October 2019).

27 Form of question to referees, J.A. Kilgour, 17 April 1929, Moore College Archives, Sydney.

28 *Ibid*.

29 *Moore Theological College Register of Students*, 14 June 1929, p.528, Moore College Archives, Sydney.

30 Copy of birth certificate of Doris Ada Hill, 19 October 1967, Walsh family papers.

31 Baptismal certificate of Doris Ada Hill, 15 March 1989, Walsh family papers.

32 *Sydney Morning Herald*, 8 November 1940.

33 *Canberra Times*, 26 March 1929.

34 *The Sydney Sun*, 27 March 1929.

35 *Truth* (Sydney), 14 January 1940.

36 *The Times Literary Supplement* (London), Vol. 1, No. 1, 23 October 1897, p.29.

37 Copyright application by Kevin Walshe, 23 June 1944, Australian National Archives, NAA: A1336, 39955.

38 *Ibid*.

39 *Ibid*.

40 Sir Norman Thomas Gilroy (1896–1977) was born in Sydney in 1896 to parents of Irish descent. In February 1946 Pope Pius XII named him cardinal, the first Australian-born man to be elevated. Much of his energy was devoted to Catholic education and by 1971 he oversaw 366 schools with 115,704 pupils. He died in October 1977 and was

buried in St Mary's Cathedral. Cardinal Freeman said of Gilroy's episcopate: 'He combined prayer and action … moving from one to the other with no pause between.' Boland, T.P., 'Gilroy, Sir Norman Thomas (1896–1977)', *Australian Dictionary of Biography, National Centre of Biography*, Australian National University (http://adb.anu.edu.au/ biography/gilroy-sir-norman-thomas-10308/text18241, published first in hardcopy 1996, accessed online 8 February 2018).

41 Colin Delaney (1897–1969) was born in February 1897 in Victoria to an Irish-born father. He joined the New South Wales Police in 1919 and 'proved an acute and skillful investigator'. Delaney was appointed police commissioner in October 1952, the first Catholic to hold the position. Delaney died in July 1969. Wotherspoon, Garry, 'Delaney, Colin John (1897–1969)', *Australian Dictionary of Biography, National Centre of Biography*, Australian National University (http://adb.anu.edu.au/biography/delaney-colin-john-9945/text17617, published first in hardcopy 1993, accessed online 8 February 2018).

42 Correspondence between Provincial and General, 5 September 1953, Christian Brothers Archives Sydney.

43 Correspondence between Provincial and General, 20 December 1953, Christian Brothers Archives Sydney.

44 Correspondence between Provincial and General, 2 February 1954, Christian Brothers Archives Sydney.

45 Correspondence between Provincial and General, 16 February 1954, Christian Brothers Archives Sydney.

46 Correspondence between Provincial and General, 18 November 1954, Christian Brothers Archives Sydney.

47 Correspondence between Provincial and General, 8 March 1955, Christian Brothers Archives Sydney. Tomás de Torquemada (1420–98) was a Spanish Dominican friar who headed the Spanish Inquisition (1483–98). Under his authority thousands of people, many of them descendants

of Jewish or Muslim converts to Christianity, were tortured and executed for apostasy and heresy.

48 Correspondence between the author and Brother Vincent Duggan, Christian Brothers Province Leader, 21 April 2009.

49 Divorce case papers, J.K. Walshe *v.* D.A. Walshe, New South Wales State Archives, series 13495, 1731/1958.

50 *Ibid.*

51 *Ibid.*

52 Letter from Father Benedict O'Donoghue to Reverend Father Romauld, 22 August 1959, Walsh family papers.

53 *Family Chapters Book*, Rydalmere, Archives of St Benedict's Monastery, Arcadia.

54 *Ibid.*

55 Prior's Council Meeting minutes, 12 September 1960, *Family Chapters Book*, Rydalmere, Archives of St Benedict's Monastery, Arcadia.

56 Reverend Walter Skehan papers, *Index of Clergy of the Archdiocese of Cashel and Emly,* Vol. 4, p.84. Cashel and Emly Diocesan Archives, Thurles.

57 Prior's Council Meeting minutes, 10 February 1961, *Family Chapters Book*, Rydalmere, Archives of St Benedict's Monastery, Arcadia.

58 Correspondence between the author and Brother Terence Kavanagh OSB, 14 April 2009.

59 *Ibid.*

60 Prior's Council Meeting minutes, 4 April 1960, *Family Chapters Book*, Rydalmere, Archives of St Benedict's Monastery, Arcadia.

61 Letter from Father Benedict O'Donoghue to J.K. Walsh, 15 November 1961, Walsh family papers.

62 Letter from American Travel Headquarters to the American Consul, Sydney, 7 June 1962, Walsh family papers.

63 Correspondence between the author and Brother Terence Kavanagh OSB, 14 April 2009.

64 Death certificate of James Kevin Walshe, New South Wales register of births, deaths and marriages, ref: 1977/006658.

Conclusion

1   Shakespeare, William, *Troilus and Cressida,* act 2, scene 2, ll. 56–7.
2   Doyle, Roddy, *A Star Called Henry* (London: 2000), p.275.
3   *Irish Times,* 9 December 1921.
4   Dowd, Christopher, *Faith, Ireland and Empire, the Life of Patrick Joseph Clune CSSR* (Perth: 2014), p.197.
5   Flanagan, Donal, *The Meaning of Knock* (Dublin: 1997), p.46.
6   *Ibid.*

ꟾNDEX